THE
LOSING
OF
GORDON

THE
LOSING
OF
GORDON

A Beacon Through the Storm Called "Grief"

Joni James Aldrich

Preface

When I was growing up in a small town on the North Carolina coast, there were no early warnings before a storm hit the area. My family and I lived through many tropical storms and hurricanes in our home. As the tempest raged, we would huddle together in a corner away from the windows. Our refuge was in total darkness, except for a few candles or lamps. The wind howled like some ungodly demon. As a result of the gale, the rain and debris pelted the house with such power that it sounded like the end of the world. We had no way of knowing what was happening in the world outside of our walls. In our isolation, all we could do was focus on our own peril.

Most of the emotions we felt were out of fear and a total lack of having any control over our fate. It was in God's hands. The roof could have blown off, windows could have exploded, a tree could have fallen on the house, or a power line could have snapped and started a fire. After hours of hell on earth, all of a sudden everything just stopped. Sanity returned, and you had time to catch your breath and survey the damage caused by the wind and water. The fact that I lived through many horrific natural disasters may be the reason that I have such strong survival skills today.

When a loved one dies, your house is blown apart by circumstances that were out of your control. And this hurricane won't dissipate in mere hours. You have to work to build a new foundation. Uncertainty, insecurity and change are constant companions. You may suffer from depression and stress. Always remember that your destiny is within you, and you are part of God's plan.

Keep searching for your beacon in the storm. Your guide will be those pivotal forces and emotions that will lead you through the difficult job of rebuilding your future.

Beacons help guide navigators safely to their destinations.

GORDON ERIC ALDRICH

Born July 31, 1960
Died May 13, 2006

Gordon was born in a small town in Michigan to Gordon and Charlotte Aldrich. Several years after he was born, the family moved to Statesville, North Carolina.

Gordon and I met in 1984 and were married on March 22, 1986. We made our home in Winston-Salem, North Carolina. Gordon continued building a successful sales territory selling utilities equipment in North Carolina, South Carolina, Virginia, West Virginia, and Georgia.

Like most men, Gordon enjoyed his "toys." We originally bought a boat, but we soon changed to motor homes. Gordon's family camped while he was growing up. We continued the camping tradition for fifteen fun years.

On May 13, 2004, Gordon was diagnosed with multiple myeloma, a rare form of blood cancer characterized by white blood cells called plasma cells. This flood of errant cells crowds out the healthy blood cells in the bone marrow, leading to fatigue, bone pain, anemia, kidney failure, and recurrent infections. Bone tumors are common; they eat your bones from the inside out until they become fragile and break.

Despite the fact that he was young, strong, and determined to beat the odds, his cancer was more aggressive than his treatments. Gordon died on May 13, 2006, two years to the day after he was diagnosed, right after our twentieth wedding anniversary.

Dedication

"*The eyes are the windows to the soul.*" The eyes are an expressive indicator that a person is going through grief. I have seen it in so many eyes, including my own in the mirror. Recently, it was clear in my friend Jackie's reddened eyes. She had lost her husband, Bob, after sixty years together. I wrapped her up in a heartfelt hug. That was my way of expressing how much I understood her pain. There are times when mere words cannot say enough.

How do you cope with such an overwhelming loss? In order to survive, you have to take your grief-stricken eyes and transform them into "new" eyes. It can be terrifying. The world is different, so you have to view and accept it differently. That's not easy to do. We look into the darkness, searching for a way through this unplanned detour affecting our future. Sometimes the eyes don't sleep for remembering and wondering.

This book is dedicated to those who have grieved and lived through it, including Jackie, Bobbie, Rita, Kevin, Kathy, Shirley, Pat, Judy, Jane, Sue, Carlene, Glenn, William, and my own mother. Some of these are cancer widows or widowers. When it comes to grief, it doesn't matter what causes the loss. Death is an unfortunate part of life.

The sky a black sphere,
the sea a black disk.

The lighthouse opens
its solar fan on the coast.

Spinning endlessly at night,
whom is it searching for

when the mortal heart
looks for me in the chest?

— from "Lighthouse in the Night" by Alfonsina Storni

This picture was taken during a recent trip to Europe with my sister. After you have experienced difficulties in your life, you learn to appreciate the incredible opportunity you have to do something as simple as wading in the Mediterranean Sea.

Table of Contents

Introduction

It took me nine years (after my young and very short first marriage) to find Gordon, two years of dating to marry Gordon, and twenty years of marriage to lose Gordon. I didn't believe that I would ever have to live without him, nor did I believe that I *could* live without him. Yet somehow after losing Gordon to his heroic battle with cancer, I picked up the pieces and moved on. I lived. This is my story. If you read *The Saving of Gordon,* I left you hanging without closure on my part. That was intentional, as the book was about our efforts to save Gordon from cancer. Now it is time for the conclusion. This book is the story of my existence after Gordon died.

It's been three long years since Gordon's death, yet I was recently reminded of my loss in an unusual way. Darn my dentist for retiring; you see, he was Gordon's dentist, too. After getting my teeth cleaned recently, the remaining dentist in that group visited to do his follow up. As I was leaving, he looked down at my chart with a "humph." I asked him what was wrong, thinking that maybe it was time to do X-rays. Then my eyes landed on the sheet he was looking at. There was Gordon's name, and it was obvious from the date that he had not been to get *his* teeth cleaned in a while. I hastened to explain that Gordon had died. Without any obvious thought at all, the dentist simply said, "That's the only excuse we allow." Needless to say, I'm now looking for a new dentist. I can't imagine anyone of character saying something that insensitive to a widow. And I am still a grieving widow.

If I had visited a fortune teller less than a decade ago, I would have been sure he or she was a fraud when they told me what would really happen in my future. Gordon was seven years younger than me. Never in my wildest imaginings did I expect him to die from cancer at such a young age. It is just as well that we *don't* know our future, because sometimes knowing the truth could rob us of our sanity.

I don't claim to be an expert on widow-ness. I've never been one before. All I can offer you is the knowledge that I've gained through experience and research, in the hopes that some of my insights and stumbles might inspire and help you along your own journey through grief.

Grief is a long process, and not an easy one. Eventually, the loss of someone we loved results in what I refer to as a "rebirth." Just like our original birth, we don't have any say-so about being "reborn." God doesn't ask our opinion. We are forced to accept that which we once believed was inconceivable.

Always remember: You are not alone! There have been many before you, and there will be many that come through grief after you survive it. And you will survive.

Author's note: Interspersed between chapters are eight Wall of Dedication tributes to special women who have lost their husbands and rebuilt their lives. These touching remembrances are directly from my heart to honor those who have moved forward into their unknown future with strength, grace and dignity.

Letter from Gordon

May 13, 2006

Sweetheart,

How are you holding up, kiddo? I know that today was the worst day of your life, because you had to let me go. I wish I could give you a big hug and kiss. Please remember that I love you.

This letter is coming via airmail. (See, I finally have my humor back.) Please don't worry about me. The cancer could not follow me here. I am free at last. I know that your pain is just beginning. Be strong.

When I arrived here earlier in the day, Dad, Mom, and Uncle Herb were waiting for me. This place is so beautiful. I cannot explain it in words that you can understand. There is no pain or sorrow. I feel only peace.

Cling to the wonderful memories we shared during our twenty-two years together. One day in the far-distant future, I will be waiting here to greet you. And, no, you were not meant to die before me. You have much work on earth to complete before you leave there. It is your destiny to share our story with the world. I will be with you in spirit.

You will always be my beautiful bride. Love,
Gordon

Chapter One:

Absence of Closure, Presence of Pain

May 13, 2006

My dearest Gordon,

There is a Cherokee expression: "When you were born, you cried and the world rejoiced. Live your life so that when you die, the world cries and you rejoice." Today, the world cried because of the loss of a "balding man with a booming voice." At six o'clock this morning, you said good-bye to the pain and suffering that you've endured so bravely over the two years since you were diagnosed with cancer. (Evidently, May 13 is the worst day of my life for two reasons—first, you were diagnosed on May 13, 2004; second, you left to be with God on May 13, 2006. This is very unfair, because it was my grandmother's birthday, which will now forever be tarnished.)

It's selfish of me, but while you're rejoicing, my pain and suffering has just begun. How can I live without you? This is not at all what we had planned! We didn't even have an opportunity to say good-bye. The cancer in your brain made you different towards me in the last weeks of your life. I know you felt I had given up on you. In some ways maybe I did, because I knew you had sacrificed so much. The very essence of my Gordon was gone forever. The cancer would have continued to steal away your dignity a little bit at a time. So this morning, I held your head and told you to go with the angels.

So, my dearest, God has seen fit to separate us for now. Things will be very different for the rest of my life. Don't worry about me, because my Mom is here to hold me up. And your sisters have been so good. Damn, it hurts so bad.

I will always love you.
Joni

You may find this hard to understand, but I don't know when Gordon died. Oh, I know very clearly that he stopped breathing and his soul left his body on May 13, 2006, at 6:00 a.m. Because he had cancer in his brain, I cannot be sure when Gordon had his last cognizant thought as my Gordon.

I like to believe that he was aware when we celebrated our twentieth wedding anniversary on March 22, which was close to a month before his "breakdown." It's entirely possible, because a CT scan that was done in February showed no sign of the cancer that had thoroughly infiltrated his brain by April.

So how do you know that your husband has cancer eating away his brain? There are signs. Whether you pick up on them or not depends on how serious they are. The weekend before Gordon collapsed, he was driving our motor home seventy-five miles an hour down a busy interstate, when I just happened to look up and saw that we were headed straight off the side of the road toward the trees. I screamed. What do men do when you scream while they're driving? They fuss and ask you what the heck is wrong. Thankfully, whether Gordon recognized it or not, that scream saved us both from what could have been a nasty crash.

The following Wednesday, we were at the cancer treatment center. Gordon was just walking down the hall, and then suddenly he was falling towards the floor. No, he didn't trip, nor did he pass out. His legs just quit working. That was a sign, but his doctor chose to ignore it.

The next morning, we met with Gordon's radiological oncologist about a multiple myeloma tumor on Gordon's upper right arm that was being treated with external beam radiation. By then, that was the least of my worries. I was trying to tell the doctor that something else was terribly wrong. Gordon was still insisting that absolutely nothing was wrong—it was simply my overactive imagination. Thank God he had to go to the bathroom. The minute he left the room, I fell apart and told the doctor that Gordon needed help. He ordered a CT scan of Gordon's brain. They immediately admitted him into the hospital. Sometimes it pays to be a whistle-blower.

I'm completely serious when I tell you that between the ground floor of the cancer center and the upper floors of the main hospital, Gordon went from what appeared to be a completely sane man to a totally unstable man with minute-to-minute hallucinations. It was that fast. Mere hours before, he had driven to the hospital. I was horrified the whole way; there were school buses on the road that morning! Yet when I expressed my concerns, he claimed I didn't know what I was talking about. Gordon was a professional driver. His brain simply could not comprehend that something was wrong, especially with his driving.

The monster that I had feared, from the very first multiple myeloma tumor in Gordon's spinal column, had finally surfaced. The brain and spinal column are both part of the central nervous system. A myeloma tumor had ruptured and sent the cancer into Gordon's spinal fluid. Although he had been receiving chemo injected directly into his spine, somewhere along the way his cancer had invaded his brain. We had never been able to get ahead of it with his treatments. Now, the disease had sent a final deathblow resulting in the loss of our two-year battle for Gordon's life. That was a hard reality to accept, because there had been many twists and turns in our cancer struggles. We had attacked each one as they occurred. Now cancer was poised to win the war.

Needless to say, it was not necessarily a big surprise when the medical team came to tell me that cancer had gone to Gordon's brain. At that point, I believe that the opportunity for us to have said good-bye as husband and wife was past. In many ways, I didn't know the person that lived in Gordon from that point, and he didn't know me.

Just recently, I had a pivotal encounter with a man who lived through a horrific car crash. For a while, his brain was mush. The accident and Chris's injuries were so bad that he had actually died several times. It's amazing that he can still talk and walk. It wasn't easy, but his survival makes Chris a living testimony to what a person thinks and feels when the brain isn't wired properly. For the first time, through Chris I was able to get a mental picture of what was going on in Gordon's scrambled brain—as painful as that was—during those final few weeks of his life. Gordon and I were married for twenty years, and then, all at once, I was married to a stranger. In fact, for some of the time during the final weeks, Gordon forgot about the cancer and thought he had been in a horrible accident. It was logical, because the onset of brain cancer had left him in a wheelchair—he had forgotten how to walk.

I actually envy spouses that have had a proper good-bye before one of them leaves to be with God. I hope that was the case in your darkest days. Some people have told me that their wife or husband told them that it was okay to move on and even okay to find someone new to be in his or her life. I was deprived of those tender moments that are often shared before a loved one passes away.

For several days after we brought Gordon home with hospice, he would ask, "Why is hospice here?" I would break down and patiently explain that the cancer had gone into his brain. Fifteen minutes later, Gordon would look at me and ask, "Why is hospice here?" Then I would go through it all again, including the crying.

Though I didn't have negative feelings towards God because of the cancer, it was difficult to forgive him for those final weeks of Gordon's life. Why were they necessary? How could all of our years together go away without loving closure? It wasn't like Gordon was killed instantly in a car wreck. He was there; he was breathing and talking, yet the words he said to me in those final weeks were not my Gordon. No matter how hard I tried to believe that Gordon was "there," he really wasn't. That was pure agony. In the years following his death, those negative memories would pollute the other twenty-two years of happy memories we had shared together.

The hospice nurses told me that death from brain cancer usually results when the patient forgets to breathe, just as Gordon had forgotten how to walk. The morning of May 13, 2006, dawned brightly just like any other pre-summer morning. Just like that fateful day two years before when Gordon was diagnosed with cancer, this morning was different behind the outward facade of the world. Gordon's life was over. My life—as I had known it for twenty-two years—was also over. Just as a country takes a long time to rebuild after a war, it would take a long time for my world to right itself. And I was not yet ready to face the necessity of the rebirth that must inevitably come for my own survival.

Dealing with the lack of closure.

"Understanding the how and why by filling in the gaps allows us to begin mending our own broken hearts, but there will always be unfinished business. We can never finish everything because grief is not some type of defined work project with a specific date for completion."

— Christine Jette, *I'm Grieving As Fast As I Can:*
Thoughts on Closure

How do we cope with the issue of closure? I recently had the opportunity to meet with several women who lost their husbands to suicide. That was a defining moment for me. When I think back at how devastated I was by the absence of the tender words of love that husbands and wives often get time to share before their separation by death, the new perspective I gained from discussions with these women that had no closure at all made me realize that some closure is different from no closure.

Looking for "closure" is a natural—but painful—part of grief. Guilt is, too, but neither of these feelings are a productive contribution to our rebuilding process. And, until we meet our loved one in a different place, facts are facts—there can be no other closure. What is it anyway? Shouldn't the twenty-two years that Gordon loved me be enough to prevent me from dwelling on the last, difficult segment of our life together?

If you can, close your eyes and visualize the "compartments" of your grief, such as pain, family, stress, and fear. One of those should be called "closure." Think of moving that issue away from the other more amenable rebuilding blocks. Store it away as non-productive. Maybe you'll return to it—maybe you won't. For now, leave it alone, until you are more emotionally equipped to focus on that elusive thing called "closure."

"God grant me the courage to accept the things I cannot change..."

Grief survival tip number one: While planning and preparing for the services, focus on getting through today. You will thankfully be in a fog. Tomorrow will come soon enough, and the emotions will contribute to your numbness.

"You have to accept whatever comes and the only important thing is that you meet it with courage and with the best that you have to give."

~Eleanor Roosevelt

Chapter Two:

It is Time to Grieve

My dearest Gordon,

We were going through pictures to add to the photo collage for the funeral. Remember the Puerto Rican Hooters' girls? Guess I better not use that one, although I really liked that big smile on your face. In most of the other photos, you had that "I really don't want you to take my picture" smirk-for-a-smile.

Today Chester and Anita came by the house to visit with me. It's funny, I knew both of them from your work, and now they have a new place in my heart. We went to dinner, where they told me that there would be bucket trucks at your visitation. I said, "I know," because we have the toy bucket trucks from your office set up by the guest register at the funeral home. They responded, "No, you don't understand. There will be real bucket trucks at the visitation." Gordon, it's the most amazing thing; I can't imagine anything that you would like better than a bucket truck arch at your visitation! What a great surprise it was. So you see, everyone misses you already. They all loved and respected you.

Many of the guys on your sales team will be your pallbearers. Bob and Lee III will give the eulogy. Although we never had an opportunity to discuss the details of your funeral or burial, I believe that you would be happy with the arrangements. I have allowed sufficient time for those from around the country to travel here to pay their respects to you. I know that you will be smiling down from heaven.

And so it begins. Eternally yours,
Joni

When we were originally told about the first tumor in Gordon's spinal column, the neurosurgeon at the emergency room said to us, "It's not time to grieve." That was a bold statement, considering it wasn't her life that had just gotten turned upside down. I can guess why she said it; I'm reasonably certain it was to yank us back out of our shock. Considering it now, I would have to disagree with her. There are many types of grief. One of them is the grief you feel at the loss of your normal life. There is no "off" or "on" button for grief. There is also no control volume for feelings.

What followed that pronouncement was two years of trying to save Gordon from his cancer. Every moment we breathed that was our stated goal—to save Gordon's life. Then like a ship sailing close to the edge of a waterfall, one day we sailed over the cliff. Time stood abruptly still and nothing was the same from that minute forward.

"It's not time to grieve." Somehow those were never comforting words. Then again, there are some horrors that transcend the ability to be comforted by words.

When Gordon was fighting his cancer, he would often ask, "Why me?" Now that he's gone, it's my turn to ask, "Why me?" Selfishly, I want to scream it. With so many unhappy marriages, why does it seem like the happy marriages are the ones that suffer through serious illness? Why did God select Gordon and me to have our happy lives destroyed? We were blessed to have it all—a happy marriage, great careers, a nice home, and the pleasure of spending time together traveling in our motor home. We had built a great foundation for our love. It fractured on a beautiful day in May 2004, and then crumbled on a beautiful day in May 2006.

My dad used to say, "Get off of the pity pot." Indeed, for much of my life, if I felt sorry for myself, there wasn't usually a good reason. Gordon and I were big fans of Zig Ziglar. On one of his CDs, Zig discussed the response that some people in tough life situations might have:

"Typically when someone is asked, 'How are you doing?' he or she will respond with some mundane, uninspired response like 'I'm doing okay,' or 'I'm hanging in there.' Of course, hanging is not real good. Sometimes they even say, 'So far, so good!' In other words, they are expecting things to get worse. Occasionally someone will say, as he pulls himself up, 'Well, under the circumstances...'—which makes you wonder what he's doing under there in the first place!"

Sometimes, we can't help getting "under the circumstances." Either way, my Southern upbringing dictates that I offer a word of greeting to those who pass through my world on a daily basis. How do you do that and grieve at the same time? When I would meet people on the street or pass them in the hall at work, I would simply say, "Morning." I couldn't say, "Good morning." After all, it really was *morning*. It just wasn't a *good* morning from my viewpoint.

Life goes on around you. That was the thing that always amazed me—immediately after the loss of my father years before and then after the loss of Gordon, I expected the world to just stop. Didn't the world know that I was terrified? Didn't the world know that I was hurting? My world had stopped; how could the rest of the world just go on as if nothing had happened?

It just does. Now *it is* your time to grieve.

When you undergo a catastrophic loss in your life, you have every right to feel self-pity. Just don't drown in it. My emotions ran the gamut from sad to angry every day. I was *finally* angry with God. I had never blamed Him for Gordon's cancer. He made a beautiful world. Humans came along and polluted it. Well, there's no proof positive as to what exactly causes cancer. In fact, cancer has been around throughout recorded history. It has even been discovered in the mummies unearthed in Egypt. Cancer had surfaced in my life and taken away the person that I cherished more than myself.

Yes, you'll be angry. While you are grieving, whack a mole, not a person. (My grief counselor, Pat, has that game in her office. We often played it at fairs during our youth. Somehow that kind of aggression transcends to us "grown ups," and whacking those moles on the head can be a great anger release mechanism.) Yes, I know your aunt June gets on your nerves. For that matter, when you're grieving, most everyone will. Dredge up some patience and know that this, too, shall pass.

When you fall off that cliff, you have two choices: sink or swim. Survival doesn't have to be pretty. Grief will leave you floating with the currents. At some point you have to find your footing. Don't focus on the self-pity, or let it rule your life. Turn your eyes away to focus on your future. Whether you like it or not, tomorrow will be a new day. I'd be willing to bet you had a life before the person you lost came into your world. No, you won't be going back to that life, but your future will be some combination of the old and new life. Just like a butterfly, you will emerge from your cocoon of sorrow with new wings.

Grief survival tip number two: Tomorrow is here, if that's possible. (Whether you think it should or not, the world still rotates.) You're deep into preparation for the services. It is time to honor the one that you loved.

"What lies behind us and what lies before us are tiny matters compared to what lies within us."

~Ralph Waldo Emerson

WALL OF DEDICATION TO

Rita

Celebrated because: There are times when no amount of love or tireless courage can save a loved one from cancer's rage. You can only do the very best you can, live every moment, and then cherish those moments in the long days that follow.

Memorial: To Chester, husband to Rita.

Beauty and Purpose: Rita continues devoting herself to Chester's mom and her own family.

Quote of honor: *"If we deny love that is given to us, if we refuse to give love because we fear pain or loss, then our lives will be empty, our loss greater."*

— Anonymous

(Note to the reader: The Chester in the letter at the beginning of this chapter was one of Gordon's best friends from work. He lived in central Tennessee, so Gordon and I often visited Chester and Rita on our cross-country trek to Little Rock, Arkansas, for Gordon's treatment. Chester was diagnosed with pancreatic cancer a year after Gordon died. It's odd, but Gordon had specifically told Chester—if he were ever diagnosed with cancer—to go straight to the best cancer treatment facility for his type of cancer. Why he said that to Chester I will never know, but a scant year later, Chester was fighting for his life at the University of Texas MD Anderson Cancer Center. He fought bravely for two years, then lost his battle to pancreatic cancer in early 2009.)

Chapter Three:
A Broken Shell

My dearest Gordon,

Last night after the visitation, we could all hear the sound that you loved—bucket truck engines—as I was saying good-bye to your empty body for the last time (it didn't even look like you). I know that your soul has flown with the angels. Your sisters were carrying things out to the car. Sherri came in and asked me to hurry outside. I did, and there was this beautiful rainbow streaking across the sky! She said at one point it had been a double rainbow, which is very rare. I hope that was a sign that you approved of everything.

By then, I thought my feet would fall off. So many people came to pay their respects to you. It was a packed house. Family, friends, comrades, and customers—they were all here to honor you. Many had traveled a long way. And you should have seen my mother at the door greeting every person that entered. What would I have done without her during these impossible days? Gordon, I could almost see that sly smile on your face. You always liked to be known, but you hated to be the center of attention. You were today, my darling, you were today.

Tomorrow is the service at the church. I so wish you were here to comfort me. Then I wouldn't need comforting.

I will love you always,
Joni

"A Broken Shell" by Joni James Aldrich

I used to roam the ocean floor
    with a life that was my heart.
We joined together very well,
    until one day you went away.

"Where are you now, my missing pulse?
    There is no life without you."
No answer here to my question,
    I drifted to places unknown.

That day, I was an empty shell
    with no power to propel me.
Then something worse took over;
    I was pulled by the tides at sea.

Defenseless against the water,
    I crashed with the tide to the shore.
Again by waves so ruthless,
    my body broken, whole no more.

Piled up with lonely other shells
    up on the sand so hot and dry.
I lay there many lonely days;
    then a kind stranger passed me by.

Suddenly I was lifted up:
    a broken shell so blemished still.
She cleaned the sand off of my back:
    "I know just what to do with you."

A broken shell still has beauty
    and with a purpose once again.
She made me part of something new,
    and now my beauty's shining through.

Not unlike humans in tough times,
   when grieving breaks their stride.
Their broken shell can be repaired
   with loving care and restored pride.

A purpose found and cause renewed
   can be our human lifeline, too.
But not unlike the broken shell
   we'll drift until we make it through.

My name is Joni James Aldrich. I'm a broken shell. Don't worry; it's not an addiction. I'm not addicted to my grief. In fact, I've spent most of the last three years challenging it.

I lost my forty-five-year-old husband, Gordon, to cancer. That was the day that I broke. How am I broken? There are several changes inside of my heart and soul. I'm not hopeless, but sometimes I sure do feel helpless. No matter what, I can't change the loss of Gordon.

I have always been a hopeless romantic, but I no longer believe there is always a happy ending. Please don't confuse that with cynicism. It's not that I don't believe in happiness. I still believe in all of the things that make happiness happen. Unfortunately, my problem stems from "always waiting for the other shoe to fall." Perhaps it stems from lack of faith in the world. I just do not trust that happiness will last. There's some part of me that understands now that life can intervene without much warning. I'm always expecting the other shoe to fall.

Just like that broken shell, there is emptiness deep inside of me somewhere. I've spent some of the time since Gordon's death filling in the gap. You'll still find it right below the surface. You see, I had built my shell hard and fast around him. That's the very meaning of being a team. Not by his choice, he left that shell forever. How do you fill the void? No glue can do it. To a certain extent, no replacement inhabitant can do it. It has to be lived with and recognized for the rest of my life. Not just a broken shell; also a somewhat empty shell.

Then there's my spirit. It's severely damaged. Oh, not the *outward* spirit that I show to the world. It's the *inward* spirit that makes and defines who

I am. I directed that loss towards God. That was futile and could not last. For a little while, though, I just could not fathom the purpose of praying for "God's will to be done" when it was going to be done anyway.

In the poem I wrote to begin this chapter, the broken shell had lost its "heart." Then it was pushed and pulled by the tide of the ocean. When you lose a big chunk of your life, you are somewhat adrift without a strong footing. Frozen. You feel "pounded" because the world (portrayed by the ocean in the poem) keeps on going around you. Because life doesn't stop, you're "pulled" along with it. And yet, there doesn't seem to be time to breathe. It all moves so fast, before you can adapt to the changes.

Thinking again about the components that make me broken, I'm out of my comfort zone. Everything around me seems surreal. Sometimes, because I can no longer touch and feel Gordon, I irrationally wonder if he ever existed at all. Well, of course he did. In some fifth dimension of my mind, I wonder. Then I feel guilty. Gordon existed very much. He was about as real as they come.

Being an "A" personality type, I don't like not having control. Yet I tried so hard to control keeping Gordon here with me; how could I just accept the defeat? Just like the shell, I was frightened for my future. Loss of comfort zone leads to loss of confidence. Most people who know me would find that hard to believe. The loss of Gordon deeply shook my confidence. I felt old, tired, ugly, and unwanted, just like the broken shell. I was resigned to living my life as a lonely widow. Who would ever want me? I was just a shadow of who I once thought myself to be.

You may notice in the poem that the shell didn't get any comfort from being one of the "lonely others." Even if you're surrounded with thousands of people, to a certain extent you are still alone. Do you find that odd? I do. It might seem different if some of the others were going through grief, but I doubt it. They would not be experiencing *your* grief and *your* sadness.

Although I have gotten it back, my smile was broken. Since childhood, I was taught by my father to have a sense of humor. Yet for at least a year after Gordon died, my smile was just a façade. It was like a mask that I put on in the morning and took off at night. If you think the smile was for show, laughter was an impossible commodity. And if you shook the tree hard enough, it would fall with a resounding thud to the ground. It required a lot of control to keep that smile in place.

In conclusion, you may as well say that I died, too, the same day, moment, and second that Gordon did. The only difference between his death and mine was that I was resurrected on earth, not in heaven. Just like a forest that has been burned to the ground, new life grows up out of the ashes. With enough love and enough faith, you can recover and become human again. It's not easy. I would never tell you that. But your recovery is essential to who you are, and what you will become.

The Story of a Shell

The empty seashells you find layered on the beach once were home to animals called mollusks. They build their shells by secreting a liquid that hardens around them. As the animals grow, their shells grow with them.

Conchs and whelks often find new inhabitants for their shell when the mollusk is gone. Otherwise, shells are prized by humans, who pick them up on the beach as we walk along the shore, and take them home like treasures.

In the grief survival tip below I refer to "beauty" in the literal sense, not physical attributes. This type of beauty is in your soul and is part of your spirit. When I mention "purpose," I'm referring to finding the drive and determination to rebuild your life and, by achieving the goals you'll find in your heart, attaining a new normal that will sustain you through your lifetime.

> **Grief survival tip number three:** Broken shells still have beauty and purpose. They will repair over time with lots of love from your family and friends.

Chapter Four:

When Mourning Comes

My dearest Gordon,

The service today was beautiful. There were bucket trucks at the church, too! Right in front. Bob and Lee III did a great job with the eulogies. Gary did a special rendition of "The Lord is My Shepherd" that I requested. He and Charlene make a great team.

As we were leaving the church, Dallas came to me and said he hadn't had a chance to say good-bye to you. You were very special to him. So I asked the funeral director to give him a few minutes with you. It was so touching and special; Dallas went up to your coffin, put his hand on it, and told you good-bye. I looked down at him and asked if he had what he needed; he just said, "Yes." He was all right after that. Sometimes we don't realize the impact that death has on children.

Tomorrow we fly to Michigan for your burial. There will be a short service there. Bill and Mary will be able to attend. Bill was devastated by your death. After your father died, he thought of you as his own son.

We leave in the morning. I'm flying on the plane with you, although the woman from the airlines that I spoke to had trouble understanding. She thought you needed a seat. I finally asked to speak to someone who could understand what I was trying to say. I admit my patience is low, so I'm sure it wasn't entirely her fault.

I miss you already. I never expected you to die first.

Much love and many kisses,
Joni

Seven realizations of grief:

1) **Grief has left a vacant seat in your life.** No one can fill that seat, but eventually the emptiness will be less noticeable and even somewhat tolerable.

2) **You are alone, but not completely alone.** You have family and friends to help. There are many others who are in similar grief patterns. Your grief may be unique to you, but not unique to the world.

3) **You must take control of your grief, or it will control you.** For a while, this will be hard to do. As time passes, your strength will build up enough to get through the crisis part of grief.

4) **It is okay to set some temporary boundaries for your grief.** I'm the type of person that doesn't say the words "I cannot." Consequently, I wanted immediate resolution for the pain, so I didn't have to admit my limitations. Grief just does not work that way.

5) **Regrets, lack of closure and guilt are your grief enemies.** These are non-productive by-products of the insecurities of loss. You will have to determine your way of dealing with them, but you can't just sweep them under the rug.

6) **In due time, you will need to reconcile with God.** Yes, I had hard feelings. Having a rift with God is along the same lines as

challenging fate. It's futile to throw your faith, hope and comfort away to be spiteful to our powerful creator.

7) **If you need help, ask for it.** Humans are not perfect. Regardless of who and what you are, regardless of how tough and determined you are—grief can knock you down. Don't be afraid to ask for help from professionals who are experienced in providing assistance to overcome some of the negative factors of your loss.

People have always died. There are different traditions to mourning, most of which we don't recognize anymore. That's a shame, because in many cases there are no outward signs after the services that your life has changed forever. Personally, I felt better at the funeral in some ways because I donned my black suit and hat (complete with black veil) with honor. It was an honor to mourn Gordon, even though I obviously would have preferred not to. The black clothes were an obvious indication that the man that I loved had gone with God.

In recent years, I have come to appreciate tradition, especially those of Native American tribes. Here is an excerpt from a Web site regarding Navajo funerals:

"First, a Navajo blanket is placed in the casket. The family provides two or more sets of clothing—one to be worn by the deceased, the second to be placed in the casket. Food, water, and items that may have been valuable to the deceased also are placed in the casket. Because of the native beliefs, everything that is made has the spirit of the maker in it, and must be cut or broken in order for the spirit of the maker to be released. The funeral service is done in both the English and Navajo languages. The items other than the clothes are placed in the casket after the funeral service and prior to the graveside service. All present must leave the church except for the immediate family, funeral directors, and minister. After the graveside service, we hold a shovel filled with soil and all people in attendance walk around the grave counter clockwise sprinkling the dirt on the casket. If the casket is a sealer casket, the end cap is not placed on or the casket is not sealed at all so that the spirit may be released. When the

grave is dug it is checked several times that no foot prints are left in or around the grave so the spirit guide will not take the wrong spirit."
—from *Releasing the Spirit: A Lesson in Native American Funeral Rituals* by Gary F. Santillanes

This caught my attention because of a recent trip to Egypt. There are holes in the side of the great pyramids for the souls of the dead to escape. Many of their other traditions are similar to those of the Navajo tribe, even though they are on two different continents.

So what are the traditions of my faith? I'm a Methodist; so was Gordon. We have ceremonies to honor the dead whose spirit has already gone to be with God. When the services are over, so is the ceremony and somehow life has to return to normal. I cannot explain it, but I almost like the old traditions of mourning. It would have been easier to don a black dress every day as the only reminder. Instead, I would often look into the faces of those that passed me in public places and wonder why they could not see from my face and demeanor that I was in mourning and had lost the love of my life. It would almost have been easier to wear the letter "M" so that people around me could see that I was extremely fragile emotionally. It wasn't because I wanted them to feel sorry for me; I just couldn't understand why they didn't *know* that I was different than they were.

Where did the illustrious term "widow" come from? How could I possibly be one? There are certainly no positive connotations to that word. Think of the black "widow" spider, aptly named because the female eats the male after they mate. Then there's the "widow-maker," a term that has been used for centuries for sailing ship parts and weapons alike.

I'm sorry; I just don't like the word. But it cuts down on conversation. If I want to explain to people that I lost my husband, all I have to say is that I'm a widow. What really cuts down on words is the silence that follows. People don't know what to say. In truth, I think that they are not expecting those words, because I'm relatively young for a widow. So the silence falls. It's a real conversation killer.

The term *widow* means a "woman whose husband has died and who has not remarried." The Latin word for widow is *vidua* and is related to "bereft" and also "to divide." So the basic translation is that a widow is a woman who is "separated" from her husband. This day and age, we call that "divorced."

Although there have been wealthy widows in literature, the image of a widow as a poor woman is more common. Several Biblical passages require succor for "fatherless children and widows." In fact, widows are mentioned in the Bible fifty-six times. The status of widows has been an important social issue through the years, particularly in the past. In families in which the husband was the sole provider, widowhood could plunge the family into poverty, and many charities existed to aid widows and orphans. Thankfully, I was financially self-sufficient when Gordon died. He made sure of it.

Another issue that many widows and widowers face is the loss of other factors in their life. For example, Gordon and I had a great ongoing relationship with the company he worked for and many of his peers. When he died, for all intents and purposes the literal bond that formed that relationship was severed. Gordon worked for and with a great group of people, so I still keep in contact with many of the people that Gordon worked with. In fact, his company sent flowers to me in remembrance of Gordon's birthday the year after he died! Can you imagine—they remembered something that so many people would have forgotten? I was truly touched.

Many things have changed and will continue to change in the days, months, and years ahead in your life. Focus on you. Not the *you* that is a widow or widower. Not the *you* that is in mourning. The *you* that I'm talking about is the one that you were before, during, and after *you* lost your loved one. That person will always be there for *you*. It is time to revisit and redefine who *you* really are.

Grief survival tip number four: After the services, there is nothing else that you can do for the loved one you lost. Now, turn the focus on yourself. Be selfish. Be aware of your feelings. Face the future with all of the strength you can muster.

WALL OF DEDICATION TO

Bobbie

Celebrated because: Whether the battle is very short or goes on for an extended period of time, the courage necessary for a cancer fight is never ending. Through the years that she has been a dear friend to my mother, I have admired Bobbie. Her spirit through Carl's illness confirmed that she is not just admirable—she is also brave and strong.

Memorial: To Carl, husband to Bobbie.

Beauty and Purpose: Bobbie continues devoting herself to her mother and her children.

Quote of honor: *"Love is something eternal... The aspect may change, but not the essence."*

—Vincent Van Gogh

Chapter Five:

To Say or Not to Say?
(to someone who's grieving)

My dearest Gordon,

I went back to work today. William (who is still grieving from the loss of his son) recommended that I get back to work as soon as I could. It's a distraction. Anyway, after only two short weeks since your loss, I faced the "world" at work today. It wasn't so bad. Everyone there is sympathetic to what I'm going through. They went through the cancer battle with us. And my best friends got me through. You know, Becky and Gloria and all of my girlfriends from work. What would I do without them? And my boss, Gary, as always, was very understanding. I'm sure he knows that my mind is just not on my work right now. It's still very hard to focus on anything except you. I live with the hope that it will get better every day. I'll just keep painting on my smile every morning so nobody will see the pain on the inside.

Being at work isn't so bad, but going home emotionally exhausted to that empty house where you died—well, it has become impossible. Some decisions have to be made...

Sure do wish you were here. Love,
Joni

The worst things to say to or about a grieving person:

"At least they (you) had time to prepare."

Whether you have ten years, ten months, ten days, or ten minutes to brace yourself for the loss of someone you love, in some ways it just does not matter. Unfortunate people who have experienced a sudden, tragic loss may disagree. Having lived through Gordon's final days, I know that the "time to prepare" may be very difficult.

It's hard for me to admit, but I've been guilty of using this phrase in reference to grieving families in the past. If I heard that someone had died, I would ask, "How long were they sick?" Now I know better. It didn't make a bit of difference that we had fought the war against Gordon's cancer for two years. We had still expected a positive outcome, which now was never going to happen.

Let me give you an example of what I mean. Imagine that you're crossing a busy street. You get into the middle of the street and suddenly hear a lot of road noise to your right. A feeling of dread comes over you. You instinctively look to the right. What you see strikes immediate terror down to your toes. There's a tanker truck coming straight for you, and you know that it can't stop in time. You can hear the tires squealing, and smell the rubber burning. You realize that there's no time to get out of the way. It's going to hit you and kill you. Right now is your time to prepare.

Is there anyone reading this story who truly would prefer to die in this scenario? Or would you rather turn a corner and be smacked by that tanker truck before you even knew it was going to happen? (Obviously, we would all prefer neither.)

Several years before Gordon was diagnosed with cancer, there was a man at work who was diagnosed with terminal cancer and died shortly after. I often wondered what his family must have been going through during the remaining weeks of his life. Now I know.

People believe that having "time to prepare" gives you an opportunity to say good-bye to loved ones and put affairs in order. True, but that doesn't change the face of what the person and their family have to go through during those last, often-dreadful days or weeks on earth. For Gordon there was great pain, both of the mental and physical varieties. There was disbelief. There was bitterness brought on by anger. We brought in a minister to counsel with him, but how can you make peace with God when you're so very angry about the course your life has taken and at such a young age?

Why was he so angry? Gordon had spent two years going through hellacious treatments, sick and in pain—now what was the result? He had spent his career saving and planning for his retirement – why hadn't he just spent that money and enjoyed it while he could? He had held back on many pieces of pizza during a multitude of different diets; why had he worried about being obese when he was going to die from cancer? More than anything else, I think Gordon was angry about having to leave me, his family, and his earthly life behind to go into the unknown. And his brain was scrambled enough that he could not reason anything out except anger.

And what about those that loved him? Agonizing, long days of feeling pain for your loved one. Days of wishing for death to come and so alleviate the suffering of both the patient and everyone around him or her. Finally, guilt for feeling that way. How can you wish for someone you love more than life to die "for their own good?"

Does this sound like time to prepare?

"Everything will be all right."

Oddly enough, Gordon used to say this to me after my father died. I hated it.

Unless God comes down from heaven and through a miracle of faith and love picks up your loved one and brings him or her back to life again, "everything will be all right" is not an appropriate phrase. There is a terrible, gaping void left by death, which cannot be filled by anyone or anything else. There is no "do over."

Admittedly, the person suffering the rebirth through the death of a loved one will probably be all right. Life goes on. There is feeling, and there is healing. Some days you think you're going to die; other days you *know* you're going to die. Always, life amazingly goes on. Finally, you know that you're going to live.

"He or she is in a better place."

Oh yeah? Have you been there? Yes, I believe in God and heaven. How can I truly know that Gordon is in a better place if I've never been there myself? I am a literal person. I've never spent *90 Minutes in Heaven*. Besides, being selfishly in grief, *I want him here with me!* And, by the way, funerals are not the time or place to convert mourners to Christianity. Some people mean well, but there is just too much shock and emotion to think of anything except for getting through the day.

"I know how you feel."

Don't say this unless you literally know exactly how the person suffering the loss feels. The grieving person may be kind enough not to say anything, but inside he or she will burn bitterly knowing that you *do not* know how he or she feels.

"He/she is tough" or "You're going to be okay."

My mother told most of the people who showed up for Gordon's funeral that I was tough and would make it. Oddly, that didn't bother me, because it was the truth, and she knows me better than anyone. Some people don't make it through grief. I even know of one person who had a heart attack after her dog died!

Years ago, a woman I worked with committed suicide on the first anniversary of the day that her son got killed. At the time, I thought, *Why did she wait a full year to kill herself if the grief was that hard to take?* After going through the grief for Gordon, I now understand about "the firsts." We'll talk about "firsts" later in the book and discuss ways to get around them. The point is, there are people who are not "tough" enough, and there are people who are not going to be "okay." So don't voice the assumption that they are.

"I wish he/she were here to see this."

No kidding. Isn't that amazing? Me, too!

"Time heals all wounds."

Unless you're prepared to state a specific time period, this is not a good thing to say. The time factor doesn't help unless you can fast-forward to the healing part.

"I've suffered through a divorce. It's a loss, too."

I would never say that divorced people don't grieve. To say that it's as serious as losing a spouse to death is not a good analogy. There are some similarities in the loss itself, but the biggest difference is that the spouse has actually died, which means there is never going to be any contact with that person in this lifetime.

"Grief is a process."

Sorry—I could care less about the process. I just wanted relief from the pain.

"If there is anything that I can do..."

Many people say this and truly mean the words. Some say it because—as they watch the grief in the other person—they want to help take the pain away. Those experiencing the grief hear the words, and believe them to be spoken truthfully. This statement is not a bad one, just be prepared to follow through on your promise.

The most comforting things to say to a grieving person:

Because I've been through a tragic illness and loss, people often look to me for guidance about what to say to friends who have lost a loved one. Believe it or not, sometimes it's best to say nothing at all. Being a good listener is a great characteristic in a friend who wants to help. Sometimes if you don't know what to say, don't say anything at all. Otherwise, the simple words "I care" are the most comforting. It's even okay to admit, "I don't know what to say."

"You have my deepest sympathy."

In your deepest, darkest hours, it is wonderful to know that people care about your loss. Even though you may think that this phrase is somewhat cliché, it is good to hear.

"You'll be in my prayers."

In your deepest darkest hours, it is wonderful to know that people care enough to think about you after the funeral is over.

"He/she is out of pain."

After a long illness or even a brief one with much pain, this is comforting to realize. While you would have wished for your loved one to never go through the pain, the fact that they did makes it comforting to realize that they aren't going through it anymore.

"I admired [the person] because..."

The fact that you remember fondly many special things about the person the family is grieving is wonderful. Don't take it too far, though. Be sincere.

Here are some other tips that are helpful:

- Never rush the grieving. Give them all the time they want with the body or at the gravesite.
- Don't encourage the grieving person to "get it all out." Grief isn't one of those life challenges where you can have a good cry, then move on.

- Don't try to find a lesson in the event. Don't say, "The Lord has something more," "It was God's will," "It was just his time," or "The Lord must have needed him more that we did."
- As the days pass following the services, don't say, "you should be over this" or "you know he/she wouldn't have wanted you to feel this way."
- Never tell grieving parents to "be grateful for the children they still have."
- Don't change the subject away from discussing the loved one.
- Don't let your discomfort surrounding the death prevent you from helping, calling, or visiting. Your avoidance will increase the confusion of those who are grieving.
- Keep your words and sentiments brief. Remember that the person receiving them is in a fragile frame of mind, and there is usually a long line of people who are waiting to offer their condolences.
- If you're not good with words at times like this don't use them. A simple hug goes a long way in conveying your sorrow and comforting thoughts.

Grief survival tip number five: Accept expressions of sympathy with grace, and try to understand that sometimes people really don't know what to say or how to say it.

Chapter Six:

Admitting That You May Need Help

My dearest Gordon,

In the final weeks of your life, I knew that I would ultimately need either counseling or exorcism—whichever came first. Those were very bad days and weeks. No offense, honey, but you were awfully hard on me. I recently met a man who had been through a severe brain trauma. He was trying to explain to me how you felt and what was possibly going through your mind during those final days. I can only hope that you are at peace now. Somehow, I have to move past that; right now it's hard to rationalize. We loved each other so much, but the line between love and hate is a fine one, and I think that in some ways you hated me in your final days. It's not going to be easy to get past that.

So, back to the subject of counseling—do you remember Pat at the cancer center? She and I were always close, so I've started going to her. Unfortunately, you know how stubborn I am. The first thing I told her was that I wanted to know exactly when I would feel better… period. Can you imagine how irked I was when she told me that grief was a process? I don't like it. It hurts. I want it to go away. She said that out of respect for you, I needed to grieve. I love and respect her, but what? Like I could stop the grief from coming! Anyway, I will be going to her for a while, or at least through the grief p-r-o-c-e-s-s.

By the way, I've just recently found out that those antidepressants that I had you taking to help during your cancer battle don't really work at all. At least the ones I've tried haven't. All they've done is cause bad side effects. Gloria has asked me to go back to the gym with her. Maybe I'll try that. It couldn't hurt my already low self-esteem. Evidently, my confidence in myself was buried along with you.

I miss you so much.
Love, Joni

They say that everyone grieves differently. That may be true, but I think that many things are the same for every grieving person. We all cry, often at very odd times. We don't always break down at the mere mention of our loved ones name. We might be sitting around eating an ice cream cone, and it will hit us. Grief is a fickle emotion.

One reaction to grief is what one widow describes as feeling like you're "running from something." It seems like you are on the move all of the time. I think this effect may be as simple as refusing to be home alone. A second possible cause may be that—if you stop, your fear is that you'll simply fall apart. In some cases, I think that it just feels good to be out and about, if you have been helping a loved one through a long term illness at home. Whatever keeps you "running," you are not alone. I found the following comments through my research on the Web:

"We lost our teenage son a year and a half ago in a tragic automobile accident. We have an older son, who just graduated high school, and we are seemingly getting on with our lives, but often, it just feels more like we are running. We stay busy day and night. It's as if we are ter-rified that if we slow down for one minute, that cold, hard, and oh-so-familiar reality will set in. We know our son is gone. Our faith tells us that we will be reunited with him. We aren't without hope, but I need to know if this constant running in order to avoid feel-ing the pain of our loss from this unexpected death is healthy or unhealthy for us?"

The response was this: "It is very normal to keep running in order to avoid difficult painful feelings when dealing with unexpected death. Keeping busy and on the go is a protective mechanism that allows your family to avoid being overwhelmed by the emotions of grief. This way of coping may be most useful in the early phases of mourning. What may have been useful early on in the grief process may not be as useful at this time. Your question suggests that perhaps you are ready to slow down, and make some time to feel the painful sadness, which you so aptly describe as the 'cold, hard reality' of your son's real absence from your daily life. Rather than worry about what is healthy and unhealthy, it is often useful to ask what it is that you feel would be most helpful to you at this time."

There are many side effects to grief. The "running" syndrome is only a concern if it doesn't diminish over time, or if you cannot stop running away. Your mind and body will let you know, if you've gone too far.

Some doctors are now studying the effects of what they refer to as "complicated grief." They call it a "condition." With complicated grief, the feelings of disbelief, loss and anguish are more extreme. This vividly reminds me of a friend whose husband committed suicide. She has had an extremely difficult time moving forward. As if it wasn't problematical enough, she found her husband dead after he shot himself. In one way she was relieved; her son had not found him. What a noble testimony to the protective instincts of a mother. And, yes, I can see how Grace's grief is very complicated.

I suffered from some form of grief amnesia. My brain wouldn't allow me to focus on the days prior to Gordon's death, as long as I wasn't asleep. If I was asleep, all boundaries were bypassed. My counselor said that your brain simply won't focus on what it cannot process. I would have to agree. While some of the horrid memories would "flit" through my brain, they would not take hold there. It seemed as though my brain was stamping them back down away from the surface.

Counseling can be a tremendous help when you're going through the most difficult time of your life. Some of the specific tasks of grief counseling include: emotional expression about the loss, accepting the loss, adjusting to life after the loss, and coping with the changes within the griever and the world after the loss. There are various types of individual or group counseling.

While I was going to Pat, sometimes I would think, "*This isn't helping!*" Pat may be a wonderful woman, but she's not a miracle worker. She couldn't just snap her fingers and take away my pain. There were many times when I left her office thinking about what she had said. Then something would happen to trigger a comment that Pat had brought up, and I would find that it was very helpful after all. She pushed me gently through my grief.

The death of someone you love is absolutely traumatic. Your family and friends won't want to live it and relive it every time they see you. Don't get me wrong—my family and friends *would have* listened and given comfort; I just didn't want to put them through it, especially when so many of them were going through their own personal grief for Gordon. His sisters had lost their mother in September, then lost their brother in May, only nine months apart! In some cases, you can lean softly, but there is a limit.

In Gordon's final days were embedded many horrific memories. I knew from the time we brought him home with hospice that I was going to need some mental guidance. During the days that followed Gordon's death, I was a wreck inside.

At the risk of stating the obvious, grief cuts us off from someone or something that gave life meaning, purpose, safety, and predictability. Severe losses leave us with a feeling that we are walking way above the ground because we have no foundation that we can touch or feel.

Phase One: Shock or Denial

The first phase of the process of grief is shock or denial. This phase protects the survivor from the emotional actuality of the death. A need to stay busy, occasional confusion, an inability to express emotion, inability to function, and an overwhelming sense that something is wrong without grasping the reality of the loss are common characteristics of this phase.

Okay, that was the official version. Let me interpret: "Hello, my name is Joni. I was going about the business of my normal life. One minute everything was fine, then—smack—I was in hell. Well, it seemed like only one minute, from zero to hell in the blink of an eye. Imagine your heart being cut into by a huge pair of scissors. Imagine your brain being frozen in shock. Imagine your nerves standing up on the very edge of your skin right under the surface. Imagine that if anyone touches you, you'll just crumble into a million distinct pieces. If I stop—even for one moment—I won't be able to get my legs to move forward again. Am I going to be like this for the rest of my life?" That's true shock and awe.

Phase Two: Expression

The second phase of the process of grief is the outward and inward expression of the grief. Bargaining, anger, and depression may last from several days to several years. There are mental, physical, and emotional manifestations that may come and go, or appear in any combination. These may include a preoccupation with the death, inability to focus, a lack of productivity, paranoia, or inconsistent thoughts. Some effects are physical, such as fatigue, insomnia, weight loss, weight gain, headaches, or other illnesses.

Okay, that's the official version, but here's the unofficial one: "Hello, I used to be Joni. Now I don't know who I am. I feel ugly and unloved. What do you call someone with no personality? There ought to be a name for that total lack of self. You see my smile? Well, this morning it took an extra hour of prep time for me to paint it on. There's simply nothing behind it. I have replaced the feeling of complete pain in every pore of my body with a total lack of any feeling anywhere in my body. See? It's empty where my heart was because it was stripped away. Out for repairs. Just not there anymore. Truth be told, I don't really care what happens to me. Blah. What does it matter? Do I look like a zombie to you?"

Just as the reality of grief is different for everyone, the emotional impact of grief are manifested in sadness, fear, anxiety, anger, depression, loneliness, confusion, helplessness, isolation, and, yes, guilt. There may be the inability to feel love or give love, compulsive behavior, or thinking that you are crazy or at least going crazy.

Phase Three: Acceptance

The third and final phase of the process of grief is acceptance. Okay, your feet will finally feel somewhat on the ground, although your legs will be shaky like a newborn colt. You will know when you have reached this stage because you will be able to recall memories of your loved one fondly and pleasantly instead of painfully. Once acceptance has been reached, planning for the future becomes reality.

Here's the unofficial version, because life does go on: "My name is Joni. Several years ago, my very existence changed. It's hard to believe. I look back on those days and wonder, *What happened?* It's almost like amnesia; that whole time in my life is like one big foggy period. Who came to Gordon's funeral? What did I do afterwards? What was I thinking? How did I get through that thing called grief? *Did* I get through that thing called grief? Who was I really during the grief process? Thank you, God, for bringing me back into the light of day from under my cloud of mourning." Relief.

From my own firsthand experience, every one of these phases in the "process" is impossible to comprehend. To me, the best way to get through is not to focus on the process itself. Today is today. Tomorrow is tomorrow. The past is past. Take it one day at a time. Grieving is hard work—mentally, physically, and emotionally. You will feel drained. You can also be very proud of yourself for every obstacle you overcome and every roadblock you make it through.

I very verbally let Pat know from day one that I didn't want to hear about a process. I just wanted to know how long the agony would last. With the loss of Gordon came other soul-bearing burdens. We had fought so long to keep him alive that when he died there was an underlying feeling of devastating *failure.* Defeat. Despair.

How had we come to be in this place? It felt like Gordon was in one universe, and I was in another. There is still a strong emotional bond between us; it's just all inside of me. That bond does not just disappear because of death. Where is it supposed to go? After a while, a new version of peace will come.

My sessions with Pat were like having a pre-scheduled meltdown. I got through the week with a fake smile, then went to Pat's office and fell apart. Then, back to the fake smile for a while. The counseling allowed me to move forward with my life without driving everyone else around me totally crazy.

Grief survival tip number six: Get out of the house. If you don't, grief will catch up with you and overwhelm you. Go out to dinner. Go to the movie. Go bowling. Join a gym. Get counseling, if you need to. It's okay to ask for help!

More about grief counseling:

Places to get private counseling—Hospitals, cancer centers, mental health clinics, hospice aftercare programs, churches, synagogues, chemical dependency inpatient and outpatient programs, schools, universities, funeral home aftercare programs, employee assistance programs, and other programs that serve chronically ill or terminally ill patients, and, of course, private practice therapists.

Other than private counseling, there is counseling available for couples, families, and/or group counseling. These sessions usually take around one hour per visit. It's amazing that investing time in that one short hour can make a big difference in your grief sanity.

Within each of us is the beacon that lights the way through the storm called "Grief." Take one small step at a time. Stretch one hand out of the darkness. One heart still beats and must survive.

WALL OF DEDICATION TO
Shirley

Celebrated because: Whether the battle is tough or impossible, it takes spirit and determination to fight against cancer. Ronnie and Shirley faced insurmountable odds, but fought diligently to overcome them. Regardless of her own physical pain, Shirley courageously cared for Ronnie throughout his cancer illness.

Memorial: To Ronnie, husband to Shirley.

Beauty and Purpose: Shirley continues devoting herself to her family, children, and grandchildren.

Quote of honor: "One word frees us of all the weight and pain of life: that word is love."

—Sophocles

Chapter Seven:

Respect Your Own Powerful Instincts

My dearest Gordon,

This past weekend was the Memorial Day holiday. Right or wrong, I couldn't just sit around the house, so I took Dallas to Disney World. Granted, it may seem an odd choice to some people. At least I was close to Tigger* there! And Dallas and I haven't had much time to spend together since we were away fighting your cancer in Little Rock. He had a great time, and there's little doubt that he needed it. Sometimes in my grief, it's difficult to remember that other people hurt from the loss of you.

You know that I had on my happy face, but you also know that you were not very far from my mind. Remember the times that we had at Disney World? Our first anniversary trip? Remember that March trip to Orlando when it was so cold we had to buy Disney sweatshirts? That seems like a million years ago.

Wish you were here to share more happy times. Love,
Joni

(*Author's note: Tigger was always my favorite Disney character. Gordon would always buy Tigger-wear for me at Christmas. This became a special part of our holiday traditions.)

Last fall, I happened to be at the right place at the right time to watch wildlife conservationists open a sea turtle nest to release the babies from their egg sacks. Half of the nest had already hatched. The other half needed rescuing. As these strangely miniature sea turtles ambled out to sea (with the path made smooth by caring volunteers), I was able to get some incredible pictures. While all of the photos were well received by the viewing public, the one that seems to have the most emotional responses is one where the baby turtle is facing away from the camera. People prefer that frame because it shows the footprints in the sand going towards the water—the babies were on the way to their new home. It was one of the most awesome experiences with nature I have ever experienced. How did these hatchlings know to go towards the ocean, even though they were only one minute old? Through instincts of survival!

When you lose someone you cherish, you are in unfamiliar territory. To a certain extent, you need to let your instincts guide you. My grief counselor commented that I was very good at determining what I needed when I needed it. I certainly was unaware of that. All I was doing was making decisions that would take me along the path I thought would be less painful. The path that I could handle emotionally.

When my father died, I promised my mother that we would take a trip to Maine. It was one place that she had always wanted to go. When she traveled with my father (which they had not done for many years due to his lengthy illness), they always went west or south. Because my father died in February, we couldn't escape to Maine right then. Mother and I were too emotionally challenged to go at that time, anyway. Early that fall, we flew into Portland, rented a car, and drove up the coastline towards Bar Harbor. I recall her commenting after viewing the first lighthouse on a rocky cliff that she had always pictured Maine this way. We continued the trek north, eating lobsters all the way, and had a great time. That trip soothed her in her grief. Mom always loved to travel. It was a life raft that she needed.

No matter what you do, the first Christmas after someone you love dies is going to be hard. I tried to tell myself to think of it as Jesus' birthday. I even dared anyone at work or around me to say the words "Merry Christmas." Of course, Christmas is a deluge of holiday cheer that begins in *September,* so that didn't really work very well. When you're thrown into the deep water of pain surrounding death, instinct can be a particularly useful tool in your survival kit. When you think about upcoming days like Christmas, Thanksgiving, Valentine's Day, anniversaries, birthdays—try to read your feelings. What do you think would make that day seem more tolerable? I always found several options, and then would select the one that had the path of least resistance. And try to remember that these holidays and events are typically only one day. Certainly it may be a very difficult day, but still it is only a twenty-four hour time period.

Another tactic that I found very helpful was this: after the day or experience is over, do everything that you can to put it out of your mind. Dwelling on painful days won't help you get through difficult tomorrows. Do not allow yourself to think, *Well, I did it this year, but I don't know about the next one.* In this case, forgetfulness is a useful trait; worrying about next year will just invite more bad feelings.

Being with friends is helpful, but you are no longer part of a "couple." You are only one person. It's normal for couples to want to go out with and spend time with other couples. Many divorced people reading this will understand. And married couples with children usually want to be with other married couples with children. People enjoy camaraderie with others who have the same interests. While it never bothered me that I was a "third wheel," there is sometimes reluctance on the part of widows and widowers to be around other married couples. Worse than that, it can feel like a knife directly to the heart. You have a tendency to be jealous that their unions are still intact. Yours isn't.

Being a widow or widower, you may have to find some new friends to spend quality time with. In this aspect, it is probably easier to be a widow than a widower because of sheer volume. The volume of widows to widowers is one-and-a-half widows to every widower for the sixty-five years and older group. At age eighty-five, the gap grows to four widows for every widower. In other words, there are more single widows to spend time with. If you're thinking about dating, the widowers have the advantage. When you're an early fifties widow, that's a different story.

You are now in the first stage of being reborn into your new life. Some aspects of it will be completely different; some will be the same, but different. There is no answer set in stone. You alone are the only one who can determine what you will need to move forward. In this you will have to trust me; one day you will emerge from the mantle of grief that threatens to overwhelm you. When that happens you will see the world with "new eyes" and a (somewhat) comforted mind. You will be a survivor. You will have evolved into someone you never would have had an opportunity to be if your life had not changed so dramatically.

Hugs, Not Drugs

We live in a time where drugs are supposed to be the answer for every roadblock in life. People take antidepressants for everything. I've never understood why people believe that an antidepressant will take away the pain of a severe loss. That makes no sense to me; once you quit taking the drugs, the problem will still be there. There is no way to mask what just is.

After Gordon died, I tried many different antidepressants to camouflage my mental and emotional pain. I thought they were the answer. The only thing I could tell they did was cause many more unpleasant side effects. One of them caused severe neuropathy in my hands and feet, just like Gordon had from taking chemotherapy!

Finally, my good friend Gloria asked me to go to the gym with her. That day changed my life. Exercise is great for your mental health. In fact, researchers at Duke University studied people suffering from depression for four months and found that sixty percent of the participants who exercised for just thirty minutes three times a week overcame their depression without using antidepressant medication. And exercise is a great way to be around and meet people. It can even be fun. Have you ever tried Zumba? It's a form of dance that is also exercise. I love it!

Grief survival tip number seven: Listen to your gut. The instinct to survive will be more prominent than the instinct to curl up and hibernate. Discuss the pros and cons of using antidepressants with your doctor.

Chapter Eight:
Your Conscious and Subconscious Grief

My dearest Gordon,

Things are progressing. There are still many decisions to make. I hope you would be proud of me for everything that I've done. I'm doing the best that I can.

By the way, they dedicated the conference this June to your memory. I went, but it was only a month after you passed away. I'm afraid I was not as strong as I should have been. Then in July, we lost Holly, Darlene, and Ronnie—all to cancer. I attended two funerals and a visitation. And, of course, your forty-sixth birthday would have been July 31. What a hateful few months this has been.

I seem to be able to persevere during the day, but for the nights I still require a sleep aid. I can control my conscious mind to a certain extent, but beware the subconscious mind. I'm still seeing Pat, and that helps.

My birthday is in August—how will I get through it, too? They say that during this first year, holidays, anniversaries, and birthdays are called "firsts." They are harder than just surviving on a daily basis.

At least we had twenty years of memories to share. They are just too painful to think about right now.

Happy birthday, darling. I will drink a toast to you. Love,
Joni

Now I lay me down to sleep, I pray the Lord my soul to keep. If I should die before I wake, I pray the Lord my soul to take.

I remember saying this little prayer every night when I was a child. Doesn't it sound simple? Yet it's very deep for a child, and I certainly never fully understood what it meant. Like most children, I had no concept of death or dying, and I certainly didn't want to think about it before I went to sleep. How many children did this prayer (which should have been comforting) keep awake at night?

Sleep was my best friend and worst enemy during the grief "process." I needed it, but I also feared it. While you can control your conscious mind to a certain extent, you have no control whatsoever over your subconscious mind. In sleep, memories can be so vivid that they are worse than going through the actual true-life trauma. Thoughts and feelings are distorted and suspended in time. While reliving the event through dreams, the cast of characters can spin off to many different unnatural and unfeeling personalities that we perceive incorrectly through sleep. Gordon would often be calling out desperately for me to please help him during the hospice days when he knew he was dying and couldn't walk.

One such dream came years after I lost Gordon. Usually, I took a mild sleep medication to help me rest and keep the "boogie man" away through the night. Due to several external factors, I had determined that I needed to wean myself off of the drug that helped me sleep. The very first night I tried to sleep without it, I had these awful nightmares that were just like reliving the final horrid weeks before Gordon died. I woke up shaking and completely traumatized, realizing that there was, indeed, something more horrible than living through those awful days of helplessness and hopelessness. Reliving them in vividly distorted detail after having successfully buried them deep inside of my soul for a year was much worse than the reality. No more. I went back to taking a dose of my medication. It was either that or have myself committed to a mental hospital.

According to a report issued by the Associated Professional Sleep Societies in Seattle, "Dreams may not be the secret window into the frustrated desires of the unconscious that Sigmund Freud first posited in 1899, but growing evidence suggests that dreams—and, more so, sleep—are powerfully connected to the processing of human emotions." The report determined that adequate sleep might support our ability to understand complex emotions properly while awake. I can second that notion. New research released by Florida State University found that "the presence of severe and frequent nightmares or insomnia was a strong predictor of suicidal thoughts and behaviors," even when other factors such as depression were controlled.

We all need sleep to survive, and dreams are a natural part of the healthy sleep cycle. When emotions are raw, sleep can sometimes lead to nightmares that will interfere with the ability to heal your heart and mind. It's okay to ask for help. Talk to your doctor and see what he or she recommends to get you through the night.

Grief survival tip number eight: Besides counseling by a qualified professional for your conscious mind, you may need help coping with your subconscious mind.

"Finish each day before you begin the next, and interpose a solid wall of sleep between the two."

~Ralph Waldo Emerson

WALL OF DEDICATION TO
Jackie

Celebrated because: Jackie was devoted to Bob for their entire life. He was the only man she ever dated, loved, and married. After so many years as a "couple," it's very difficult when you suddenly find yourself alone.

Memorial: To Bob Stone, husband to Jackie.

Beauty and Purpose: Jackie continues to be the strong, confident lady that she has always been, and is learning to function as a self-sufficient woman.

Quote of honor: *"The dictionary of scripture describes the eagle as: A symbol of the holy spirit, which flies, as it were, through the mind (air) from the higher nature (heaven) to the lower nature (earth) and soars aloft to the self (sun)."*
—from the Eagle Spirit Ministry

Chapter Nine:

The Business End of Grief

My dearest Gordon,

You know the plan we discussed regarding the house and motor home if anything happened to you? Well, I didn't handle things exactly as we had discussed. It was more of a guideline, wasn't it?

I have to sell the house. Even though you wanted me to keep it, it's too big, and you died there. It is no longer a "home" without you. Mostly, it's emotionally challenging for me to stay there. So I went looking for something smaller and more practical. Townhouses are too much like apartments. Then I found this charming cluster home. It's a convenient distance from everything in town. I really like it. I made an offer and they accepted.

Then there's the situation with the motor home. Just as we had discussed, I talked to the dealer about selling it and getting a smaller one, but when they came up with the deal, it would have been a huge loss to trade down. So I paid a friend to take it to the lot in Hilton Head. I'll decide what to do with it later. Now the Clerk of Superior Court says I have to pay it off before we can close the estate! That would be devastating. I'll figure something out.

Oh, by the way, it would have been nice if you had told me you changed over the cable payment to e-bill. Another day, another challenge.

Obviously, you're on my mind. Love you,
Joni

There ought to be a law. Well, technically I guess there is—but laws should be reasonable. Yes, I know that the motor home is technically a motor vehicle. I don't think of it that way, because it's considered to be a second home on tax returns. Imagine my dismay when I was told by the Clerk of Superior Court Estates Division that I had to pay off all of the motor vehicles before they could close Gordon's estate! (No wonder so many widows I've known in the past end up trying to sell their motor home right after losing their husbands.) Talk about devastating! We're talking about a hundred thousand dollars worth of motor vehicle. Thankfully, the Yukon and Volvo were both paid off. Small comfort.

The motor home loan with our bank was in both of our names. In fact, the bank didn't have a problem and couldn't understand why the court did. Gordon's will clearly made me sole beneficiary of the estate. So what was the big deal (besides the obvious outlay of cash)? Well, the interest rate of the loan on the motor home at our bank was around five percent. That was the rate when we bought the motor home new. Since we bought it in 2004, it was considered used, and refinancing would have carried a much higher interest rate. Ka-ching . And interest rates were a lot higher. Ka-ching. Even after getting a lawyer, the Clerk of Superior Courts office was continuously harassing me—not only did they show no remorse or sympathy, they even sent a sheriff's deputy to my house with a summons!

My mother worked for the estates division of the Clerk of Courts office in my home county—also in North Carolina—until she retired, and she had never heard of anything like I was going through. She couldn't understand why they didn't just leave the estate open and do a yearly inventory until I could get the matter resolved without excessive cost. The lawyer suggested that very thing. He asked the deputy clerk whom it would bother if we temporarily resolved the matter that way. The clerk replied, "It's more work for us." What ever happened to helping widows and orphans?

This persisted for almost two years after my lawyer got a temporary "stay of execution." Then, the economy finally dipped (well dropped), and I saw my opportunity to refinance the motor home in my name. I was so relieved. However, I still can't believe the emotional trauma those representatives of the state put me through. In fact, I thought about running for Clerk of Superior Court in our county, since it's an elected office. My grandfather was Clerk of Court for twenty-five years, so I would be holding up a noble tradition in our family. If by some miracle I was elected, I would go into the Clerk's office and *clean house.* Of course, I had better things to do with my time. I sincerely hope that you have a better experience when you are settling your loved one's estate.

No matter how "prepared" everything may seem, you are in the shock of mourning and everything that follows mourning. Money is the least of your worries, yet you have to be concerned with it. Funeral services and burial arrangements all have a financial impact that can be significant. If you're lucky, the lost loved one will have made his or her arrangements in advance, but that doesn't happen all the time.

- ✓ There is the cost of the funeral.
- ✓ There are still the regular, everyday bills.
- ✓ You have to take care of things with the bank.
- ✓ Money may start coming in from life insurance and so forth.
- ✓ You have to consider any outstanding debt.
- ✓ There is business to conclude with the state. (I had to *pay* the Clerk of Courts office close to eight hundred dollars for that mental abuse!)
- ✓ Don't forget Social Security.
- ✓ You'll need funds for any life changes you want to make.
- ✓ And if your spouse was working, you have to consider the lost income.

Gordon's services were both beautiful and impressive to honor him as the person that he was. These included the visitation and funeral in North Carolina, and then we flew to Michigan for another small service and his interment. Not that I'm complaining, but there can be some high costs involved in providing the very best for the one you love.

I was blessed to have the support of both of our families, Gordon's company, and my own work. While it took time to get my feet back on the ground, I didn't have the extreme issues that some people have after a catastrophic loss. I was very aware that I still had a big house and motor home, and I was down to one income. So even though everyone says not to make big decisions for a year, I felt I needed to make some changes for my best interest (and mental health).

Though I had always loved our house, Gordon had died in it. Just being alone within those walls gave me a really uncomfortable feeling. I couldn't explain it, but I knew that it wasn't good for my finances or me to keep the house. It was a big responsibility that I couldn't justify keeping. So the house went on the market, and I downsized to my little cluster home. It's usual for me to push ahead once a decision is made, so no surprise that the move was fast-paced and furious. To this day, I still can't decide what I did with some of our stuff during the downsizing process. I will admit that in this situation everything happened too fast. Truthfully, I think I felt if I slowed down, the thoughts and emotions would catch up with me.

Then there was the motor home. This took some major consideration. Gordon and I had a lot in a motor home resort on Hilton Head Island in South Carolina that we loved. It was owned by his parents and had been passed on to Gordon and then to me. In his final days, Gordon had his sister trying to put the final details together to be sure that it would be mine upon his death. I couldn't part with it. Naturally, the motor home was a big financial responsibility. Gordon had expected that if anything happened to him, I would trade it for a lesser unit that would be more economical and easier to handle. In fact, we had both discussed that possibility with a friend at an RV dealership where we had done business in the past. When I went to them, it became apparent that I would lose a lot of money by trading down. So my options were to keep it or sell it outright. Another complication was the fact that the resort in Hilton Head only allowed motor homes. In other words, trading down to a more manageable fifth wheel that could be left on the lot as a permanent structure was not an option. Since I was unprepared emotionally to go much further with that thought process, I paid a friend to drive the motor home to Hilton Head and put it on the lot. I still have the motor home and our lot. And circumstances in my life *did change.*

I'll tell you without hesitation that these decisions were not easy to make. Facing change upon change upon more change—you can only get your "arms around" just so much change. I'm an analyst. When I put everything together on paper, I came up with solutions that were a fit for the situation I was in. You have to be practical. I had resources available, but I had lost greater than half of my yearly income when Gordon died.

Believe it or not, things could not have worked out better, even though I'm not sure Gordon would have wanted me to go the same route. I sold the house just before the real estate market crashed. I love my new, smaller home, which I made comfortable in my own style with warmth. I kept the motor home, and now I have someone to share that lifestyle with. Right or wrong, things settled at their own pace and in the best way.

> **Grief survival tip number nine:** When it comes to finances, weigh all of your options. They say not to make any big decisions in the first year after the death of a loved one, but after you've carefully considered the facts, you should make the decisions that are right for you.

"In the important decisions of personal life, we should be governed, I think, by the deep inner needs of our nature."

~Sigmund Freud

Chapter Ten:

Knowing Your Limitations

My dearest Gordon,

I've been so worried about Max since you died. He's just been wasting away since you've been gone. Yes, he's sixteen (how many is that in cat years?), and we knew he wasn't in the best of health since that last trip to Little Rock. I just can't deal with yet another loss right now. Please encourage Max to keep going (from you it will have more clout).

The other cats are doing well. And I bought another kitten. He's the brown tabby I wanted when we got Mulligan. You would have laughed your head off—I called everyone I knew before I bought him, because I just know that people are going to call me the "cat lady." I don't care. It makes me happy, and that's important right now. And Mulligan needs a playmate. Max is getting old, and Calloway is antisocial. Wish you were here for bringing home the new baby. I still love those pictures with you holding Mulligan as a kitten the first day we brought him home. He was crying like a baby; then you picked him up, and you both fell asleep in the chair. By the way, Mulligan isn't so little any more. Think how big Ziggy was, then multiply that by two. And who knew that black cats were so bizarre?

We miss you (even the furry residents). Love,
Joni, Max, Calloway, Mulligan, and Palmer

Sky diving. Scuba diving. Bungee jumping. Walking on a tightrope. Living in Antarctica. Hiking in Australia. Climbing Mount Everest. Performing in Carnegie Hall. Running in a marathon. I'm not one to accept limitations, but I know that there are limits to what I want or can feasibly do. In essence, no one—and I do mean no one—knows you like you know yourself. This is important, because no one—and I do mean no one—can get you through your grief except for you.

Could I sky dive? Certainly. It's just not something that I really want to do. *Could* I sing at Carnegie Hall? Certainly. No one would pay to hear it, but I could do it. There are things that work for some people, but not for others. We are all unique. When you're going through grief, it's good to understand and respect your limitations, but don't let them define you or hold you back.

Your instincts may drive your grief limitations. A friend used to rent a house on the beach every summer with her husband. After he died, she hasn't been able to go back. Going there was something they did *together*. If she owned the house, it would be hard to avoid. Since her wants and needs aren't complicated by ownership, the desire to avoid being there *alone* is understandable.

One of my big emotional limitations was resolved by selling the house. There were others that remained. Spending time in the motor home was difficult, since it was Gordon's "baby," but there was no way to avoid it altogether. Staying alone in the motor home at the resort in Hilton Head for the first time was very difficult. Without the house, I felt the closest to Gordon there. The more I did it, the easier it became. I adapted to my limitation.

Limitations come in large and small packages. There's a great ice cream joint in Hilton Head that Gordon was addicted to. I love ice cream, too, but not enough to go there.

I taught Gordon to love cats. I was never partial to dogs, because I was attacked by one as a child. We usually had several cats at the time, mainly because of me. I always felt that cats should live in cat "families." Of all of our cats, we loved our Himalayan, Max, the most. He traveled with us everywhere. Pet owners will understand that, after eighteen years with the family, a pet is almost another one of your children.

Following our last trip to Little Rock fighting Gordon's cancer, Max wasn't in very good health. When I took him to the vet, at first they told me he had liver cancer. I freaked; I didn't need another cancer battle. Then we found out that he had cysts that would continue to fill up his kidneys and liver until they wouldn't be able to function anymore. After a round of antibiotics for hepatitis, Max revived to somewhat normal. That was good, because by then I had my hands full with Gordon.

During the awful weeks before Gordon died, Max camped right under his hospital bed. People that own cats will tell you that usually they'll be *on* the bed, especially when one of their "humans" is sick. Oddly, none of the cats got on the hospital bed that much, or even seemed to know the man that was lying there. After years of gently loving our cats, Gordon had even forgotten their names. But Max was always close by.

In the month after Gordon's death, I thought I was going to have to do the humane thing and put Max down. He had stopped eating and was skin and bones. He was dragging around the house. When I moved into my new place, he rallied. It's a good thing, too, because if I had lost Max that early in the grieving process, I simply would have curled up into an emotional ball and succumbed to my grief. Almost as if he knew that, Max fought to live. But it was the oddest thing—he would lie on the rug at the front door for hours at a time. It was like he was waiting for Gordon to come home.

Max lived for two more years after Gordon died. I still believe that he did that for me; he knew I couldn't stand another loss. When he died, I was at peace because I knew that Gordon was waiting in heaven to take care of him.

Grief survival tip number ten: Define and understand your limitations; sometimes you can even conquer them. And do whatever brings you even a glimpse of happiness during the mourning period.

Gordon was a gentle and kind man. This picture was taken the day we brought our new kitten, Mulligan, home for the first time. Gordon and Mulligan took this nap together at our home in North Carolina in August of 2005. Gordon's cancer took a critical turn shortly after this tender moment, which led to his death less than a year later.

Chapter Eleven:
"If Only" Regrets

My dearest Gordon,

I keep thinking about what we could have done differently to fight your cancer. What decisions would we have made if we had been able to see into the future? Of course, it doesn't do any good now. What would have happened if we had gotten to Dr. Tricot in Little Rock sooner? Why didn't I push harder? We never could get ahead of your cancer. Would it have made any difference, or was it just fate?

The more widows and widowers that I talk to, the more I hear the words "if only." We all seem to be cursed with the same regretful mode. Isn't that sad? Yet who can say if we had chosen different paths that the result would have been different? After all, fifteen hundred men, women, and children die from cancer every day in this country alone! Do they all make incorrect decisions, too?

Anyway, my darling, I know that you are not in pain where you are. The cancer isn't eating up your body anymore.

I sure do miss you. Love,
Joni

Psalm 55:22 — *Cast thy burden upon the Lord, and he shall sustain thee.*

My first experience with "if only" regrets as part of grief was when my father died. Dad had spent much of his life in pain. He was among the troops that landed in Hiroshima soon after the atomic bomb was dropped in World War II. My uncle tells the story about his squadron finding a can of peaches that were obviously contaminated with radiation. They ate them anyway because they didn't know any better. In the mid-1980s, Dad's duodenum (part of the stomach) ruptured. For months it was misdiagnosed as a pinched nerve in his back. By the time his problem escalated, Dad was in the intensive care unit for three months and went through five life-or-death surgeries. One surgery was to amputate his leg up to his hip.

Through the years after that trauma, Dad was never in good health. Finally, my mother called, asking me to come home as soon as possible. Dad was ill and in the hospital. Gordon was traveling, so I didn't wait for him to get home. I did, however, take Max with me. By the time I finally drove into town on that cold February night, I decided not to stop at the hospital. I was tired, and Mom wasn't at the hospital, so I reasoned that Dad would be resting and the kitten would freeze if I left him in the car alone. And I had been driving for five hours straight. I would wait to see Dad in the morning.

That was not meant to be. The call came to the house shortly after midnight. When we got to his room, it was obvious Dad was in horrible pain. No one ever said so, but something happened with his stomach. He died shortly after that. I will always regret not going into the hospital as soon as I got into town.

Most people who have lost a loved one feel some degree of guilt. We tend to blame ourselves for something we did or didn't do, or for things that we wish we had or hadn't said. Some grieving souls become obsessed by their feelings, and it overshadows moving on with their lives. Guilt is a strong emotion that affects people suffering a devastating loss because they are in an extremely vulnerable state.

None of us can live in close proximity to another person and love them deeply without hurting that person in some way. We all do and say things we later regret. When a loved one has died, we are reminded of those hurts and issues, real or imagined; of words we regret saying, incidents we'd like to forget, actions we'd like to take back.

Guilt is usually not satisfied with explanations or reasoning's after the fact. Often we feel helpless in our guilt because there is little that we can do to correct the situation. It is important to express these feelings to a family member or friend who will listen without being judgmental.

There is absolutely no way that I could have known that my father was going to die that evening. Obviously, if I had known, I would have moved heaven and earth to be with him. So how do we get over those powerful words "if only?" "If only" implies regret and a desire to go back and take a different path. The words "if only" are emotionally driven. I wish I could caution you to not obsess about the "if only" regrets, but I cannot, because I have spent hours lost in my own "if only" statements. How can I tell you not to punish yourself with "if only" when I myself have landed on the "if only" sword? Reality bites, but it is what it is.

So we need a new plan to get rid of the "if only" brain torture. Here is what I want you to do:

> Take out a blank sheet of paper. At the top, the header will read "My If-Only List."

> Begin to make a comprehensive list of all of your "if only" regrets. Take your time and be thorough. No "if only" too big; no "if only" too small for this list. They are all pertinent.

> After you have completed the first draft of the list, leave it for a while and go do something else. If you're like me, once you're away from the list for a while, other "if only" thoughts will surface that need to be added.

> When your list is complete, I want you to hold it facing upward with both of your hands towards the sky and pray this prayer: "Lord, here are my 'if only' burdens. They are abusing my mind, heart, thoughts, and spirit. I know they are not good for me. Please take them into your care. Thank you, Amen."

> After you have prayed, open your mind and imagine God's hand coming down from the clouds of heaven and taking all of the "if only" burdens off of that piece of paper. As far as you are concerned, the page is now empty.

> ➤ Tear up the "empty" piece of paper and dispose of it with fervor. There are many ways of doing this. Throw the (biodegradable) pieces into the ocean. Flush them down the toilet. Bury them in a deep hole in the back yard, then plant a nice gardenia over them. Make it a ceremony. Play rock music or Beethoven's "Moonlight Sonata." Celebrate the fact that your "if only" burdens are now in a much better place.

> ➤ This process may take several applications before you are rid of all "if only" thoughts. Eventually, they will no longer be a burden to you. They now belong to God. Be sure to thank him for taking them away and relieving your mind.

Believe me, I know it's not always this simple. If you're a very patient believer, over time your reassurance will blossom like a new spring, and you will realize that those "if only" statements were preventing you from moving on with the rest of your life. They were holding you back and therefore were unhealthy. Now, they are just where they need to be. So, drop the "if" in "if only," then remember this new statement that is more appropriate for your mental health:

"ONLY God."
Thankfully, God has great big shoulders.

Grief survival tip number eleven: Only God can heal your "if only" burdens. Let Him take them away from you.

Chapter Twelve:

What Defines You?

My dearest Gordon,

Well, I did it. I moved into my new place today. I just love it. I've decorated it all in southwestern style to my own specific taste. Maybe I'll make a buying trip to Arizona and visit your Aunt Peg while I'm there. Perhaps over Labor Day; you know how hard the holidays are. We always took trips in the motor home on Labor Day. Remember the trip to Wyoming? You refused to take more than two weeks off, so we had to hustle out there and back in only thirteen days. We had a great time. Those were the days... .

Anyway, I've moved. Now I have to get the old house ready to go on the market. I have to say, you're not on my favorite-person list right now. Remember the storage shed out back? You made a big mess out there. Sherri and Dean came over to help. Did you have to leave that big tub of oil in the middle of the floor after you changed the oil in the motor home? If you were here, I'd kick you in the knee. Of course, you didn't expect to get sick and leave me with this mess. In my rational moments, I remember that.

We'll just keep hauling stuff to the dump. Wish you were here to help. It would serve you right!

Love (even today),
Joni

If you have lost a spouse or friend, then you had a life before you met that person. If you have lost a child, then you had a life before you gave birth to that child. If you have lost a parent or sibling, then you probably developed a life away from them after you were grown. Now that this very important person in your life has passed on, how do you salvage your inner self without that person?

When Gordon and I were together, we usually listened to country music because that's what he liked. I like most types of music, so it was an easy compromise. When Gordon died, I rediscovered my love of many different types of music, including the opera that I now enjoy. Being with someone for so long means that you adapt to some of the other person's likes and dislikes, even above your own. It can have some fascinating benefits, if you explore some of those long lost interests. Music is soothing to me.

Another example is my mother. My dad disliked it when she was reading while he was watching television. Go figure! So she learned to crochet. Since my Dad died at sixty-four years old, my mom has read a library full of books. She loves to read. For her (and for me, too), television is usually on, but it's just background noise.

Fortunately or unfortunately, after I lost Gordon one of my pleasurable outlets was shopping. And I do it very well. Shopping offers immediate positive gratification. And if that new dress or pair of slacks looks good on you, it can add to your confidence level. If your shopping gets to the point of addiction, then it can lead to negative issues, especially at the end of the month when you get your credit card bill. So when you shop, remember to use discretion regarding the amount that you indulge in.

Another positive distraction that can also lead to personal growth is going back to school, either for a degree or just to take some classes at your local community college. While you're grieving, there is much to be gained by having a preoccupied mind. My counselor, Pat, returned to college and got her degree after her husband died at a young age. She has used her education and knowledge to help other people in need. You don't necessarily have to go to this extreme. Take some financial planning classes, cooking classes, a decorating class, or learn how to build a Web site or use the computer. If you work, just take a few classes at the time. Anything that distracts you and gets you out of the house at the same time is of great value.

As you rediscover new interests and pastimes that you enjoy, don't feel guilty about it. It isn't a curse or some kind of sacrilege to the one that you lost. You have been forced to redefine yourself. You didn't control your destiny. Now, you'll have to look deep inside yourself to find your true "new" center. Without the other team member in your marriage partnership, there is only one person left to keep things going forward. It's a heavy responsibility, especially in gender-specific roles. Many widows and widowers have a difficult time adjusting.

Gordon and I had a pact when we got married. I took care of everything in the home because I was better at it and he traveled. He hated laundry; when we were dating, I could always tell that it was laundry day because Gordon's usually upbeat mood would go down the toilet. I only let Gordon cook once. He assured me that he had worked in the "mess hall" during his college years. Evidently, that was a very messy "mess hall!" They used a lot of grease. After that one breakfast experience, we decided that I would do all of the cooking and he would clean up. Fairly soon after that, Gordon began to find ways to get out of that, too.

Cleaning the house didn't suit Gordon either. I recall one Saturday when he and I split up the housework. He had the living room. Several hours later, I returned to the living room to find him still sorting through a stack of motor home magazines. Yes, he had discarded a few, but he was mostly reading them. He didn't want to throw away one that might have an important article that he would need in the future!

Then what was his contribution to our marriage? Gordon handled the finances. That was a job he could do even when he was traveling. So what was my "weakest link" when I lost Gordon? The finances. Of course, I could take care of the day-to-day stuff. Income taxes were farmed out to a good friend, who also happened to be a tax accountant. When it came to retirement funds, investments and life insurance annuities, I needed help.

Gordon had established an account with the Charles Schwab investment firm. After the "dust had settled," I gathered all of the information and marched down to the local office. That poor guy must have thought I was crazy; I waltzed in and plopped everything down on his desk. I pronounced myself a widow and him the financial expert, and proceeded to tell him to do his job. While Joe took over the work itself, he put together a complete financial proposal to discuss before it was implemented. Suffice it to say that we developed a good business friendship and worked well together. While it was a somewhat risky move—don't try that with every financial firm; they may not all be as upfront and accommodating—I knew where I needed assistance and went for it.

After losing my husband at such a young age, I knew the importance of having an up-to-date will and living will. Just weeks after Gordon died, these documents were signed and sealed.

On a more personal side, a change of scenery in your house may prove helpful. Just as I bought my new place and surrounded myself with warm things that I liked, my mother did some redecorating in her house after my dad died. Even if it's just changing around furniture, painting a wall, or some other household project, making your home your personal refuge can be helpful and fulfilling. Recently, a newly widowed friend told me she spends most evenings in the den staring at her husband's favorite chair. So I asked her what would happen if she had it reupholstered or moved it to another location? I gave Gordon's favorite chair to some of our friends for their mountain cabin. I knew I couldn't give it away to just anyone; it still carried his familiar smells. By giving it to the safekeeping of our friends, it was out of my immediate vision and still had a good home.

As you move on with your future, there will be some things that you can change to make life a little easier and to give you confidence and purpose. There are also going to be some things that you can revisit from your past life or some new interests that you've always wanted to do. These will all get you moving forward into your new life. Just stay away from skydiving!

Grief survival tip number twelve: Surround yourself with things that make you happy. Rearrange the furniture or paint the walls. Changing things may give you comfort and confidence.

"You cannot teach humans anything. You can only help them discover it within themselves."

~Galileo

WALL OF DEDICATION TO
Jane

Celebrated because: Jane is an inspirational woman who has lost much in her life to cancer, including her husband Robert. And that was after she had lost her father and mother to this terrible disease.

Memorial: To Robert, husband to Jane.

Beauty and Purpose: Jane has devoted her life to her family and her second love, genealogy. What I like the most about her is her kind, gentle spirit.

Quote of honor: *"From our ancestors come our names; from our virtues, our honor."*

—Proverb

Chapter Thirteen:

Single Again and Lonely, Too

My dearest Gordon,

Surely you remember that I told you I never wanted to be single again. You weren't supposed to ever leave me. Tonight, I went out with my friend Rebecca. Wow, are things different now than they were twenty years ago. I never did "single" very well to begin with. And now I'm out there again. Honestly, not only am I not emotionally up to it, I lack the energy and confidence to face going out. What a pain, in every sense of the word. The guys all have baggage— some from divorce, some from divorces (that's plural), some have kids (I don't know if I have the energy to do that again), and the others appear to be just plain messed up. Well, I'm one to talk; obviously I have my own baggage. Dating a widow can't be easy.

It's not important. I'm okay financially, so I don't need anyone to take care of me. If I never have another person in my life, that's okay. So be it. I had the greatest guy in the world for twenty years. What more could any one person ask for? When I think of how many divorced men there are out there, it seems so unfair that you had to leave me since we were so happy! But you're gone, and it sure would be nice to have someone to bum around with.

Thanks for the memories, honey. We had a good thing. There will never be another you no matter where I look.

To my one and only love,
Joni

In the best case scenario, dating in the twenty-first century might include Internet relationships, reality shows, matchmaking services, or speed dating over lunch. In the worst-case scenario, if you make a "mistake" these days, the result can be much more than an unexpected pregnancy. And we see enough crime shows on TV to scare us into paranoia, and steer us away from even the possibility of meeting someone new (who might turn out to be a serial killer). The world of dating is terrifyingly surreal.

It's no wonder that many people who find themselves unwillingly single again in their "middle" age don't even wade in the waters of dating. Is our reality to be alone for the rest of our life? Or are we doomed to post multiple personalities on an Internet dating site like Stockard Channing in the movie Must Love Dogs?

Vince Gill once recorded a song with a line something like this: "I never knew lonely, until I lost you." I used to think it was a beautiful song. It seems that now that I can relate, I could not have said that better.

What if we take the word *alone* apart and make it grief-healthy?
A is for All
L is for Love
O is for On
N is for No One
E is for Else (but me)
All love on no one else but me.

It's time to be a little selfish. Learn to love yourself again. While Gordon had cancer, he was the china doll. Now in my grief, I am the china doll.

When reviewing other books on grief, many focus on help from others to get you through your grief. To a point, their assistance is a necessity. Unless others can be with you all of the time, the reality is that you will have to survive through believing in yourself.

While I can't tell you that being alone after losing your spouse and best friend is very fulfilling, it is something that you will need to grow through. I'd also like to tell you not to be afraid of your alone time. It takes some getting used to. Focus inward and be productive. Stay busy. Develop a social life, even if it requires some effort to keep a smile on your face.

Dating can be a very sore subject. You may or may not want to ever find someone new to spend your life with. It isn't always necessary; some widows and widowers are satisfied just living out the rest of their lives alone. My mother is one of these women. She just settled right into her life as an independent woman.

If you decide that you want to date again, there are some pitfalls (lots of them) you should be aware of. Here are some helpful tips:

- ❖ Try not to feel like you are "betraying" or "cheating on" your spouse who died. I believe that Gordon wanted me to go on, and he wouldn't have expected me to be alone for the rest of my life.

- ❖ Dating a widow or widower is not easy. The singles out there aren't the only ones with "baggage." You are still in love with the person you lost and probably always will be. Now that I have someone in my life, I find it hard sometimes to love Gordon and Doug both at the same time. Then there is the very intense emotional impact of dating a widow or widower. Emotions overwhelm us at odd times. When you expect us the break down, we don't. Yet we may turn around and cry uncontrollably during a movie. Anyone that spends time with you should expect the unexpected.

- ❖ Don't be afraid to "introduce" the new person in your life to your lost loved one. Okay, don't do this right away, but the time will come. Doug has read my two books, so he knows Gordon very well. In many ways, this is helpful in our relationship. Sometimes Doug will read something and ask, "Did you really do that?" He's both interested and involved.

- ❖ Go slowly. You will feel your grief throughout your life, but it will get easier with time. Don't force the issue. Let a new romance happen naturally. Doug and I sat across the table having dinner together with other people for six months before we went out as just friends.

❖ Give yourself permission to be happy. As human beings, we are not meant to live in caves away from other people. Humans thrive on social relationships.

Grief survival tip (aptly) number thirteen: The singles scene is not for widows or widowers right after their loss. Allow plenty of time to heal before trying to jump into this scary adventure. I recall a saying from Alaska, where there are five times more men than women: "The odds are good, but the goods are odd." Until you can sort through the "weeds," stay away from the "garden." And, by the way, this is not the solution to filling in the gaps in your life that the loss of your loved one has created. Learn to stand on your own two feet or find an expert to help you in areas that you are weak.

"Each day is a new canvas to paint upon. Make sure your picture is full of life and happiness, and at the end of the day you don't look at it and wish you had painted something different."

~Author Unknown

Chapter Fourteen:

Careless and Reckless

My dearest Gordon,

I fell down the stairs. At first, I thought I had broken my neck. You know I've always been a klutz! Well, maybe that magnum of wine I drank may have contributed to that missed step. You can't judge too harshly, because I seem to remember a two-Chianti night on Ocean Isle Beach.

In all honesty (and I have to be honest with you now that you're an angel), I think I've become reckless in my grief. In some way, I feel like I'm going around in a fog. Maybe they should suspend your driver's license, when you're going through mourning! All kidding aside, it reminds me of Mom breaking her foot so badly just a short time after Daddy died.

I promise you I'll be more careful. A broken neck is a little more serious than a broken foot!

Love you,
Joni

Depression moods lead, almost invariably, to accidents. But, when they occur, our mood changes again, since the accident shows we can draw the world in our wake, and that we still retain some degree of power even when our spirits are low.

—Jean Baudrillard

People that are grieving the loss of someone they loved are particularly at risk for depression. That's no shock. After experiencing an initial episode of depression, they are at an even higher risk of experiencing a recurrence of depression, including bouts of overwhelming sadness.

Sometimes a depressed person may experience symptoms such as a profound loss of interest in their normal activities. Other symptoms include changes in appetite and sleep patterns. When people become depressed, they can become restless, irritable, and agitated. If the depression is not treated, it may become extreme. This can lead to a feeling of worthlessness, hopelessness, or extreme guilt about an insignificant event that they cannot change.

The "Social Readjustment Rating Scale" was developed by Thomas Holmes and Richard Rahe at the University of Washington School of Medicine. The scale was based on the theory that good and bad events in a person's life can increase stress levels, and make them more susceptible to illness and mental health problems. Guess what the highest number of points is for?

If more than one stressful event has happened to you within the last twelve months, the point value adds up. (You really don't need a Ph.D. to tell you that.) For example, in the last twelve months if you have experienced the death of a spouse (100 points), and a personal injury (53 points) your total would be 153. Listed below are some of the life events on the "scale" that could closely affect those that are grieving the loss of a loved one:

- Death of a spouse (or child—this wasn't included, but it must be a high number) add 100 points
- Death of a close family member, add 63 points
- Personal injury or illness, add 53 points

- Change in the health of a family member, add 44 points
- Change in financial status (such as the loss of an income), add 38 points
- Death of a close friend, add 37 points
- Change in living conditions, add 25 points
- Revision of personal habits, add 24 points
- Change in residence, add 20 points
- Change in recreation, add 19 points
- Change in social activities, add 18 points
- Change in sleeping habits, add 16 points
- Change in the number of family get-togethers, add 15 points
- Change in eating habits, add 15 points
- Single person living alone, add 14 points

You can see that many of these could add up during the grieving process. What is your total? A change in your life requires an effort to adapt, regain stability and therefore maintain health. The higher your score, the more effort and diligence you will need to get back on stable ground.

If your score is below 149, your stress level is not that bad.

If your score is between 150-200, your stress level is still reasonable.

If your score is between 200-299, you're in the danger zone.

If your score is above 300, then you need to watch out!

Here are some common symptoms of stress by category:

Physical: Frequent colds or flu, headaches, trouble sleeping, muscle tension, skin problems, trouble with digestion, sweaty palms, indigestion, cold sores, rashes, shortness of breath, sleeplessness, oversleeping, fatigue, nausea, diarrhea, tight muscles, low back pain, ulcers.

Mental: Poor concentration, forgetfulness, frequent negative thoughts, poor judgment, disorganization, fuzzy perception, confusion, lack of interest, diminished creativity, disorientation, negative self-talk, inability to think logically.

Emotional: Anxiety, depression, anger, irritability, feelings of helplessness, a lack of purpose, relationship troubles, moodiness, humorlessness, abrasiveness, hostility, nervousness, tension, sarcasm, selfishness.

Behavioral: Eating problems, *driving recklessly,* poor peer relationships, abusing alcohol or drugs, *being accident prone,* destructive, showing aggression.

If you remain in high stress situations for a long time, the body forgets what to do when it is not in the stressful mode.

I became increasingly curious—does grief cause us to be careless and reckless? Are accidents and injuries common when people are grieving? I decided to ask that question to the general public.

Other true stories of careless and reckless behavior during the grief process:

"My father died when I was sixteen, and in June of that same year I hit a brick wall–literally! I was driving my father's car to pick up something from the pharmacy. My foot hit the gas instead of the brake, and I crashed into the brick outer wall of the building. I remember crying and screaming that my father was going to be so upset. The guy that came out to help me said, 'He won't be that upset with you, if you tell him it was an accident.' I blurted out that my father was dead."

– from Leslie

"John, my husband of thirty-three years, pulled off to the side of the road and died suddenly of a massive heart attack. Three weeks after he died, I was at the gym, but the sadness was so overwhelming that I decided to go back home. As I was pulling into the garage, I hit the side of the house, and ran into John's car. I rammed his car so hard that it went through the back wall of the garage. I realize now that I was having a complete meltdown in my grief."

– from Kathy

"I've only had three automobile accidents in my entire life. Two of them occurred twenty-four hours apart, several weeks after my mother died. The first was at an intersection, when another driver ran a red light. The second was a seven-car pileup on the freeway. I wasn't injured either time. Even though I thought I was operating at peak efficiency, in retrospect I now realize that I was in a daze. I could have avoided both accidents, if my awareness had been functioning properly. I was fortunate not to become a statistic at that time, and I made it a point to be extra careful during another period of grieving later that year."

– from Mike

"Following the death of my wife of fifty-six years, I had two careless accidents within six months of each other. The first happened about six weeks after she died. My wife was always so neat; I was trying to organize some files in the office. As I was carrying a box down the stairs, I tripped on the carpet on one of the steps. I managed to grab the handrail to stop my fall, but my ankle and hand were injured in the process. Several months later, I was cleaning up limbs around the roof and gutters. I lost my balance, and fell to the road below. This time, I had broken my big toe and messed up my rotator cup. I was lucky it wasn't worse. That was enough—I was more careful in the future."

– from Glenn

"When my forty-five-year-old brother, John, died suddenly after a brief illness, his wife called my parents at 2 a.m. to let them know. My parents—both age 82—drove two hours to upstate Pennsylvania in the middle of the night, and got very little sleep over the next couple of days as they arranged for the funeral. My mother began experiencing chest pains. Once medics arrived, the crew told my dad he could ride in the ambulance, but they didn't know where they would be taking her. Once they were settled, he wouldn't have had a ride back. So my dad decided to follow the ambulance in his car. Within minutes, he crashed into a pole. Thankfully, no one was injured, and my mother survived, although she had a 100% blocked artery and could not attend John's funeral. I believe that—if my mother had not had the attack before the funeral—the stress of attending the funeral might have triggered a far worse heart attack, perhaps even one that was fatal."

– from Jean

"My husband died right after our seventh anniversary. He had been sick with colon cancer for four years. In the year that followed, I had several injuries. My family suggested these were my body's way of refusing to stand on my own two feet. The first Mother's Day after Paul died, I twisted my right ankle when the heel of my foot slipped out of my sandal. It was a hard day, and I was in a fog of sadness. Thankfully, the injury was minor. Then I injured my other ankle, when I went away for the weekend of what would have been our wedding anniversary. I was raw with grief and trying to keep it together by creating a new anniversary ritual."

–from Sima

You are not alone…

In many ways, I think when a person you love more than yourself dies, you sometimes feel that you don't care what happens to you. If my mother reads this, she will either be horrified or completely understand. After the loss of my father at sixty-four, my mother was out cleaning the muddy ditch behind our house and broke her ankle so severely that it hurts her to this day. She had never even been out to the ditch before that I remember. Why was it so important for her to clean it that day?

In my grief, I made mistakes. I was reckless. These are all natural by-products of grief. Then I fell down the stairs and hit the side of my neck on the solid wood stair rail. That landed me in the emergency room to see if my neck was broken. For several days, they actually told me that my neck was cracked. Stupidity doesn't usually run in my family. Grief is an odd bedfellow. In a lot of ways, that fall woke me up. It scared me enough to realize that I actually *did* care what happened to me.

It's not that you would intentionally do anything to yourself. If you did, you would have to face your loved one in heaven to explain why you gave up, when he or she tried so hard to live. I could never have faced Gordon. And should you ever contemplate any self-destructive behavior, seek help immediately. God took your loved one from you, but He left you here for a purpose. That may seem unfair. It isn't our job to second-guess God.

Here are some tips for getting you through your "fragile" rebuilding period:

Manage your time – It's okay to stay busy, but don't overbook or overwork yourself to the point of feeling frazzled. While you may wish otherwise, there are still only twenty-four hours in a day.

Exercise regularly – Regular exercise will help your self-esteem, get you out of the house and doing something productive, and focus your mind away from your grief. Exercising boosts your brain's output of chemicals that counteract the effects of stress hormones.

Get adequate sleep – Getting a good night's sleep is very important. You will feel less "foggy," have more energy, and will be less prone to sickness or accidents.

Eat a healthy diet – On a recent visit with my mother to one of her doctors, he told her to "feed her brain." Certainly it's good to eat a low-fat, high-fiber diet that includes plenty of fruits, vegetables, legumes and whole grains. He also suggested at least one serving of fish every week, lots of greens (turnips, collards, mustard greens), and nuts (walnuts, hazelnuts, pecans).

Be assertive –"Yes" is a lovely word, but sometimes you have to say "no" when you're attempting to manage your stress level. If you've reached your physical or emotional limit, just say "no."

Relax – Even if it's for only a few minutes a day, find some time to kick back. I've never been fond of meditation, yet I think that it does have some healthy benefits.

Learn – Find a way to occupy and expand your mind. Think of something that you've always wanted to do and *go for it*! Maybe you've always wanted to learn more about computers, or something simple like cooking. While online classes are okay, it's better to take a class where you'll have direct contact with other human beings. We're never too old (or sad) to learn something new. And learning leads to healthy interaction with others.

Grief survival tip number fourteen: Be mindful of signs of self-destructive behavior in your grief. That can be as simple as not paying close enough attention to your driving. And I like a glass of wine or two, but excessive use of alcoholic beverages is not recommended.

WALL OF DEDICATION TO
Grace

Celebrated because: So what is in a name? The meaning of the name Grace is "Grace Of God." As I think about the woman named Grace that I met today, the name identifies a strong woman who has been forced to survive the trauma of her husband taking his own life.

Memorial: Without actually knowing him, I know that Grace's husband was a good man. Some force beyond his control drove him to do the unthinkable. He is now in God's comforting hands.

Beauty and Purpose: Some roads we choose. Some roads are chosen for us. Grace never had a choice in her road. We all have an innate dislike of things that are out of our control, especially when the results are tragic. It takes a lot of human fortitude to keep going. Grace embodies that strength, although sometimes she does not see it.

Quote of honor: *"It is only through letting our heart break that we discover something unexpected: the heart cannot actually break, it can only break open. When we feel both our love for this world and the pain of this world—together, at the same time—the heart breaks out of its shell. To live with an open heart is to experience life full-strength."*

—John Welwood

Chapter Fifteen:
Overcoming the First Blue Christmas

My dearest Gordon,

Well, they're finally here: the dreaded holidays. Christmas was always a special time for us. This year, you won't be here to be my Santa. It will definitely be a Blue Christmas without you.

I've taken several steps to try to make it easier on myself. At first, I refused to celebrate it. Next, I asked my sister if it would be okay to take Mom away on a cruise. We leave Christmas Eve. I know that running away isn't the answer, but it's unrealistic to just pretend the holidays don't exist. Everywhere you go all things Christmas-like just smack you right in the face.

After I get back from the cruise, I'm going to get together with your family. I bet little Noah has grown.

Please don't worry. I'll make it through the holidays and everything else that comes up. I really, really, really wish you were here to cut down my tree, smoke the turkey, and be my Santa.

Merry Christmas, sweetheart. Love you,
Joni

I called them the horror-days instead of the holidays. And I had to dredge up every ounce of my sanity to make it through them.

Christmas was Gordon's and my favorite holiday. It had evolved over the years as a very special time for us. We had many cherished traditions. Since most Christmas trees come from the North Carolina mountains, we would go to a farm to choose and cut our very own tree, usually one that was way too big. I would spend days decorating it by tying each of the ornaments on with ribbons. The rest of the house would be painstakingly decorated in every nook and cranny. Our Christmases were filled with family and friends that we loved, and many special memories to cherish.

We didn't have children together, so Gordon always thought of himself as *my* Santa. Every year on Christmas Eve, he would go out into the shopping madness to buy my presents. He liked to wait until the last minute because it put him in the holiday spirit. Most of the gifts weren't expensive, but each one was specially selected for my pleasure. On Christmas Eve after I went to bed, he would set up everything under the tree and fill my stocking. That had been my parents' tradition when my sister and I were growing up. Gordon gave me many enchanting Christmas mornings to remember.

As I approached the Christmas of 2006 alone, I had no Gordon to share the holidays with and to be my special Santa. As you might expect, I knew that I had to lean heavily on my family and friends. My instincts were also telling me to *run*. Yet after missing so many Christmases with my family while we were away fighting Gordon's cancer, that didn't seem right. My gut was still saying *run*. So I called and asked my sister if it would be all right if I took our mother away on a cruise for the holidays. She understood what I was going through, so she agreed.

Mom and I sailed away on Christmas Eve. I thought I was very clever until the ship's crew came to the solarium at midnight and sang Christmas carols. I just sat there with tears streaming down my face hoping that the video cameras would stay away from me. The rest of the tears I left for after we went to bed because I didn't want Mom to know. Well, of course she knew—I'm sure she went through all of this after my father died.

Running and *forgetting* are two entirely different things. *Remembering* and *surviving the memories* are different matters. I can tell you what worked for me. I was bound to feel pain and grief for Gordon (and still do) during the Christmas holidays. Amazingly, Christmas Eve seems to be the hardest for me, even during that first Christmas. On Christmas Day, all I felt was relief that it was almost over. Your experience may be different, but the facts remain: you are the only one who can get you through the painful memories and stress of the holidays. Feel your way through the path of least resistance for you. If I had a "secret formula" to make it easier for you, I would offer it. Unfortunately, there isn't one.

One more suggestion—grief counseling. Many charitable organizations have free grief counseling sessions prior to the holidays. I went to these meetings after my father passed away. You should consider it, if for no other reason than to realize that you are not alone!

Grief survival tip number fifteen: Your first Christmas without your loved one will be traumatic no matter what you do. Even on a cruise ship in the middle of the western Caribbean, I couldn't completely escape. But it sure did make it easier, especially with my mom by my side. The support of family and friends is very important.

"What is Christmas? It is tenderness for the past, courage for the present, hope for the future. It is a fervent wish that...every path may lead to peace."

~Agnes M. Pharo

Chapter Sixteen:
Recognizing Your Rebirth

My dearest Gordon,

Most people say that Sunday is the hardest day for widows. For me, it was always Friday night. You traveled during the week and came home to me every Friday night. So after you died, I started going to this little restaurant close to work. It's owned by a nice family. The owner comes to my table after she finishes for the night, and we talk over a glass of wine or two.

After a while, it became a tradition. Then, several of my friends started going there on Friday night with me. The restaurant had a wine tasting, and we met another group of people that went to dinner there on Saturday nights. So we merged the groups. Anyway, there's this guy named Doug who was in that second group. He sat across the table from me for six months without giving any indication of his interest in me—I think he could see through my "mask" of grief.

When we met, Doug was dating someone else. They broke up, and we decided to go out to dinner several times as just friends. I've planned a trip to Hilton Head for the Easter holiday. He asked if it'd be okay if he went with me. Do you think that's okay? He's a very nice guy, although he's not like you. I think for me to ever fall in love again, that person would have to be a Gordon clone!

Anyway, Doug owns his own business. Did I mention he's very nice? And he's funny. He makes me laugh, and that's something that I haven't done in a long time. I don't think you would want me to be alone for the rest of my life.

I still love you, of course, and always will.
Joni

I have been blessed to know many widows and widowers. Some of them come from the cancer experience. Some are acquaintances from the resorts in South Carolina and Florida. Some are new friends like Glenn, the eighty-two-year-old man with a thirty-five-year-old heart that I met on the beach in North Carolina. Why are all of these associations a blessing? Why is it so special to know these champions who have been reborn through the grief process? Every one of them has his or her own story to tell. Every one has a unique appreciation for living. They each have strength in a special way that others who have not "walked in their shoes" cannot fathom.

Still, I cannot tell you that they have all completed the rebirth journey through mourning. Some have a harder time than others. What these men and women all have in common is a sensitive heart and commendable spirit. They will trip along their journey through grief. They may even fall, but they'll get up and bandage their wounded hearts.

Sometimes they're hard for me to talk to. After all, my sensitive heart still has a deep gash. However, I treasure every member of this society of grievers for many reasons, this one most of all: they loved and gave of themselves to another. That trait is lacking in the world.

> **"The difference between perseverance and obstinacy is that one comes from a strong will, and the other from a strong won't."**
> —Henry Ward Beecher

Why do I call the grief process a "rebirth"? Here is the literal definition:

➢ Rebirth is the regeneration of something that has been destroyed.
➢ Rebirth is the revival of ideas or forces after a broad and significant change.

When we are born the first time, we do not have a choice. We are born on the day that it is preordained for us to come out of the womb. We have no choice about where we are born or in the selection of our mother, father, siblings, or circumstances. Our birth is a miraculous gift from God, although situations may not be perfect throughout our lifetimes.

Just as with your original birth, your need to be reborn through the grief process is not your choice. While *destroyed* may not be the correct word, you have certainly suffered a severe loss that has left you in need of personal regeneration. The forces of life and death have left you undergoing a significant shift in your lifeline. Whether we believe it immediately or not when the change or shift occurs, we all have deep within us survival instincts that have been documented since humans first walked the earth. These are the tools—the building blocks—that will form the bridge over your grief.

So what were the "tools" that helped me?

✓ Instinct concerning what I personally needed to get through my grief.
✓ Wisdom gained through prior difficult experiences.
✓ Love from my family and friends.
✓ A sense of humor.
✓ The ability to sort through and analyze critical factors in my survival.
✓ Realizing that I needed outside counseling for perspective.
✓ After a while, restoration of my faith in God.
✓ The confidence to define my future, including new interests and projects.

Our path through life is destined by God and through fate. What we make of our rebirth is of our own choosing. You can choose to stick your head in the sand and let life pass you by, or you can choose to take baby steps forward into the unknown future. While I find it difficult to have the optimistic viewpoint of some authors regarding grief and the loss of a loved one, I truly believe that every "trial by fire" we endure and persevere through in our life makes us better, stronger people. So just as new growth is reborn out the devastation of a forest fire, so grows our soul through painful life experiences.

Grief survival tip number sixteen: Sometimes unexpected things will happen in your life. Try to live and laugh again. ***Don't forget: Jesus was also reborn.***

"The only way of finding the limits of the possible is by going beyond them into the impossible."

~Anthony Robbins

WALL OF DEDICATION TO
Martha

Celebrated because: First and foremost, because she is my mother and I love her dearly. I also admire her for the life she built for herself in the eighteen years since my father died. When Gordon died, she was a beacon leading me to courage. After all, she had survived; so could I.

Memorial: To Alphonso (A.H.), husband to Martha, father to Theresa and Joni.

Beauty and Purpose: The name Martha originated from the Biblical "marta" which translates to "lady." My mother is a true lady. Now in her eighties, she still volunteers at her church two afternoons a week.

Quote of honor: *"Motherhood: All love begins and ends there."*
—Robert Browning

Chapter Seventeen:

More Than Angels…

My dearest Gordon,

Well, it's been almost two years now since I lost you. Things are going well. As a matter of fact, I finally got the estate closed. The motor home is now officially mine. It's still down in Hilton Head. I think of you every time I step into it. It was your dream motor home, and it's still just as beautiful. But I'll never forgive you for the black and gold paint on the outside and the black awnings! I tried to tell you that would be hard to keep clean.

Doug and I are still dating. He has become an important part of my life. And—would you believe it—he has taken to motor homing almost as much as you loved it. We took our first trip outside of Hilton Head after the Christmas holidays. (By the way, it was easier this year, but I still missed you terribly.) We went to The Great Outdoors in Titusville, Florida. Remember we camped there on the way to Disney World with Mom years ago? Well, you wouldn't believe it; we enjoyed it so much that Doug and I are going to buy a lot there. It's on the fourteenth hole of the golf course and backs up to a lake with our own alligator. Guess I have to make sure the cats don't get loose!

I suppose you're wondering how I'm going to do that and work. Here's the next thing you won't believe: I'm going to quit my job and write books about *our story. The first one will be called The Saving of Gordon. It's going to be about our journey trying to save you from cancer. I truly believe that our story needs to be told. It is my greatest wish that our experience would inspire others to be empowered while fighting their cancer. The second book will be about my rebirth after losing you.*

Every now and then I slip up and call Doug "Gordon." He just gives me a kiss.

I will always love you and miss you, but my life has to go on. And God has seen fit to bless me with someone to share more camping memories with.

Love always,
Joni

Artist: Diamond Rio
Title: "I Believe"
by Skip Ewing and Donny Kees

Every now and then soft as breath upon my skin
I feel you come back again
And it's like you haven't been gone a moment from my side
Like the tears were never cried
Like the hands of time are holding you and me
And with all my heart I'm sure we're closer than we ever were
I don't have to hear or see, I've got all the proof I need
There are *more than angels* watching over me
I believe, I believe

That when you die your life goes on
It doesn't end here when you're gone
Every soul is filled with light
It never ends and if I'm right
Our love can even reach across eternity
I believe, I believe

Forever, you're a part of me
Forever, in the heart of me
And I'll hold you even longer if I can
The people who don't see the most
Say that I believe in ghosts
And if that makes me crazy, then I am
'Cause I believe

There are *more than angels* watching over me
I believe, I believe

My friend Shirley can "feel" her husband, Ronnie: *"I think that the most important part of acceptance of a spouse passing away—if you ever do accept it—is being able to talk with his or her spirit. I can remember that I would sit on the bed and ask him to put his arms around me and let me know that he was there. I actually could feel his warmth and love around me, and feel his arms on my body. It is not as strong now, but believe it or not I can still feel him with me when I need him the most. As I am typing, I feel him with me at this moment. It is a wonderful feeling, yet scary."*

I'm jealous; I never experienced anything like that with Gordon. Perhaps it was because I had so many painful memories during the months after his death, that *any thoughts* of him were just too painful. So I may have shut out some wonderful possibilities for closeness to him.

My mother recalls that my dad would play tricks on her after he passed away. Rather than being romantic, he was determined to have fun even from heaven.

What are angels and how to they come to us? Do they visit us only when we let them in? Is it possible to love an angel when you can't touch it, but it can touch you? When it can see you but you can't see it? I'm beginning to sound like a philosopher.

The Bible speaks frequently of angels (for example, angels giving messages to Mary, Joseph, and the shepherds; angels ministering to Christ after his temptation in the wilderness; an angel visiting Christ in his agony; angels at the tomb of the risen Christ; the angels who liberate the apostles Peter and Paul from prison); however, it makes only two references to an archangel, Michael, in Jude 1:9 and I Thessalonians 4:16, where the "voice of an archangel" will be heard at the return of Christ.

So are angels just messengers? Evidently not. Read the information below that I found on www.bibleprobe.com/angelinlebanon.htm.

> Soldiers in all of Israel's wars have reported seeing angels on the battlefield. During the Yom Kippur War, a lone Israeli soldier in the Sinai led a captured Egyptian column back to Israeli lines.

When the Egyptian officer was asked why he surrendered an entire tank column to a single Israeli soldier, the Egyptian officer replied, "One soldier? There were thousands of them."

The officer said the rest of the "soldiers" had melted away as they approached the Israeli lines. The Israeli soldier reported that he was alone when the Egyptian commander surrendered to him. He didn't see the army of angelic warriors. The Egyptians did.

Psalm 68:7 — *The chariots of God are twenty thousand, even thousands of angels...*

In its existence, Israel has fought back invaders in five major wars aimed at its annihilation, against impossible odds exceeding six hundred and fifty to one in some cases. Israel's victory in the War of Independence was nothing short of miraculous, as were her victories in 1967 and 1973 against the combined might of the Soviet-backed Arab Legions.

Given her precarious geography, with enemies on three sides and her back to the sea, the Arab armies should have cut through her like a hot knife through butter, but amazingly, each victory left Israel in possession of more land than she had when attacked. And in every war, there are reports from both sides of angelic intervention on Israel's behalf.

No matter what your religious persuasion, these accounts are intriguing. Are they proof that angels exist?

I am going to tell you the hardest story that I can put into words. This is the absolute truth about the final minutes of Gordon's life. Before I tell it, I'll let you know in advance that, no, I did not visually see any angels. In truth, if they were there when Gordon died, I would not have known because I was focused on him.

Gordon fought valiantly, even in the days following his brain seizure from the full brain radiation for the cancer that had now overtaken many areas of his brain. There were many visits by a hospice nurse preparing us to expect the end at any time. During the final week of Gordon's "life," he slept with his eyes open. That was particularly disturbing to me. We put him on oxygen even though there was a "do not resuscitate" order.

The night of May 12, one of Gordon's sisters held one of his hands all night, and I held the other. His other sister slept fitfully on the couch just a few feet away. Gordon was surrounded by love. Truthfully, none of us got much sleep. In the early hours of the morning, we woke to the sounds of irregular breathing. I can't put that sound into words, so you'll just have to believe me when I tell you that it was inhumane to hear. In shock, I stood up and went to turn his oxygen off. Still, the breathing from Gordon's chest continued. We listened for several more minutes. During the previous days, I had told Gordon several times that it was okay for him to "go with the angels." Then he had rallied, because it wasn't his time. This time, I held Gordon's head in my hands and somehow, through my uncontrollable crying, told him once again that it was time to go with the angels. Almost instantly, the breathing stopped. Gordon was gone with the angels. It was almost as if he needed for me to tell him that it was okay to go with them. I can't impress on you in words how indescribable that was. I believe that Gordon's body was already gone, but his soul was waiting for me to let him know that it was okay for him to go.

If you talk to many people who have been with a loved one in the moments prior to their death, I'm sure you could write an entire book of "unusual" occurrences. Do I believe in angels? You better believe I do. I can't substantiate the accounts from the Israeli battlefields, but I can tell you I believe that the angels took Gordon home to be with God. His battle was over.

While I haven't been aware of any personal visits from angels since Gordon died, I can assure you without any doubt that God had everything to do with the writing of both of my books. There have been many instances where I wake up in the morning (just like I did this morning) with book ideas running through my head. This morning, I knew that I needed to write about angels. Why is that so odd? I still take something to help me rest at night and to keep the dreams away. Oh, I studied dream therapy in college, so I know that I do dream. A person will go crazy if they don't. I never recall any of the dreams. So it surprises me that in the first minutes of waking there are these "thoughts" I need to write. Doug often wonders why I do most of my writing in the morning or after a walk on the beach. This is why: ideas and thoughts just come to me.

During the final days of writing *The Saving of Gordon,* I was pushing to get the final chapters over to the editor, but I just wasn't happy with one of the chapters. Writing is an art, and sometimes it's hard to push. During the early morning hours, I got up to go to the bathroom. Believe me, after taking my sleep aid, I am really groggy when I have to get up during the night. Then a single word came into my mind: *volunteers.* The chapter I was working on was about defining of resources. I had never even thought of "volunteers" as one of the subtexts. Yet this word came to my mind out of nowhere in a semiconscious state. Other than that one word, there were no others. I somehow "felt" pleasure with the way that I was planning on restructuring the chapter. Then I went back to bed.

In the morning, I had this sense of euphoria. I was not alone in my mission. Of course, I had always known that. Did an angel speak to me? Was it Gordon trying to help me along? I have to say, if I did indeed get a message from an angel, the bathroom does seem like an unlikely place. This is my story, and I'm sticking to it.

In the book *90 Minutes in Heaven,* Don Piper describes the clear memory of someone holding his hand in the demolished car after his accident. A minister had come to pray for him and had had to climb through the trunk of the car just to get close enough to put one hand on his shoulder. Everyone thought he was dead. Almost a year after the accident, others convinced him that it would have been completely impossible for any human to be able to hold his hand in that car. In fact, they had to take the roof off to get him out. Yet he still vividly remembers that physical contact.

During one of the first meetings with a book publicist, the owner of the company told me that it was unheard of for an analytical personality such as myself to write non-technical books. Makes you stop and think, doesn't it? Yes, I'm a very goal-driven person. But if you had told me five years ago that I would write and publish two nonfiction books, I would have told you to seek psychiatric help. And since you're reading these words, you are in the process of reading what I consider to be my second miracle.

"Myriads of sounds so filled my mind and heart that it's difficult to explain them. The most amazing one, however, was the angels' wings. I didn't see them, but the sound was a beautiful, holy melody with a cadence that seemed never to stop. The swishing resounded as if it was a form of never-ending praise. As I listened I simply knew what it was."
— Don Piper explaining his heavenly experience in *90 Minutes in Heaven*

"Thorns and stings
And those such things
Just make stronger
Our angel wings."

— Emme Woodhull-Bäche

"When babies look beyond you and giggle, maybe they're seeing angels."
— quoted in *The Angels' Little Instruction Book* by Eileen Elias Freeman

"Silently, one by one, in the infinite meadows of heaven,
Blossomed the lovely stars, the forget-me-nots of the angels."
— Henry Wadsworth Longfellow, *"Evangeline"*

"You'll meet more angels on a winding path than on a straight one."
— Daisey Verlaef

"I saw the angel in the marble and carved until I set him free."
— Michelangelo

"Ever felt an angel's breath in the gentle breeze?
A teardrop in the falling rain?
Hear a whisper amongst the rustle of leaves?
Or been kissed by a lone snowflake?
Nature is an angel's favorite hiding place."

— Carrie Latet

"Have you ever seen a flower down?
Sometimes angels skip around
And in their blissful state of glee
Bump into a daisy or sweet pea."

—Jessi Lane Adams

"While we are sleeping, angels have conversations with our souls."

—Author Unknown

"When God places something that you must do into your heart, He will send
along a host of angels to help guide you through the completion of His resolve."

—Joni James Aldrich

Grief survival tip number seventeen: Be open-minded about the angels. Around the bend in the road, heaven may send you a sweet experience.

Chapter Eighteen:
Preserving Your Precious Memories

My dearest Gordon,

I hope you will understand that this is my last letter to you. It's been three years now, and it is time to move on.

I've found a new way to store my precious memories of you. After you died, I saved many of your belongings in what I call your "memory box." It contains your personal items such as your cell phone, glasses, BlackBerry (or as Justin called it, your "crack" berry), cards from you—you get the picture: all sorts of things. Now I've had another idea that I hope to share with others who have also lost loved ones.

The Saving of Gordon will be published soon. I'm so proud of it. You know it wasn't easy. It took everything inside of me to make that happen. From time to time I think, Why am I not just riding off into the sunset? Now it dawns on me that our story will live forever, even when it comes time for me to leave this earth. And don't worry: I remember all of the marketing lessons you taught me—about people doing business with people and how you always said that if you generate enough energy, the sales will come. You see? Pat was right. You may be gone from the earth, but you are alive and well as a part of me.

Please remember, just because I won't be writing to you does not mean that I will ever forget you. How could I, when I've written two whole books about our journey together? Our twenty-two years together were the greatest years of my life, although there is always room to make more memories. I think you would have liked Doug. He understands that you will always own a big piece of my heart.

Love you, darling, now and forever. Your loving wife,
Joni

So how to can you preserve and display the memories from your loved one?

There are limits. One of the mourning traditions from the past that I find a little creepy is hair jewelry or mourning jewelry, which involves making jewelry from the hair of loved ones who had died. It was popular from the time of the *memento mori* (remember me) jewelry of the Middle Ages through the sixteenth and the seventeenth centuries, and even through the nineteenth century. Truthfully, they're not that bad, so I don't know why they affect me negatively. Who am I to say whether it was helpful or not to those in mourning? It was like keeping a small "piece" of the person who was lost. In our society, the material *possessions* of a person are sometimes kept as mementos.

The thought process started when a friend of mine showed me that she had made a beautiful Christmas tree in a shadow box made out of old jewelry. After successfully completing one of my own, the thought occurred to me that I could make something similar with some of Gordon's jewelry and other jewelry that reminds me of things he loved. A long time ago one of my friends gave me a small, unique angel pin. It was different because the angel was sitting on top of a motor home. I also have a pin of an angel playing golf (although I doubt that the angel would use the same words that Gordon did while he was playing golf). I have gathered these together in a memory box in the shape of a heart (see the picture after the chapter).

You will need:

1. A shadow box—whatever size corresponds with the pattern that you want to use.
2. Background material for the bottom of the shadow box. I used decorative paper, but you can also use wrapping paper or cloth.
3. "Mementos" in jewelry from your loved one or from your own jewelry box. These should include hearts and other things that remind you of that person in some way. For instance, if they liked horses, include horses. I used a lion pin because Gordon was a Leo.
4. A pattern to follow—I suggest either a cross or heart, but you can use your imagination.
5. Wire cutters
6. Glue (use the multipurpose glue that dries clear)
7. Several hours of your time to spend remembering your loved one.

Start by gluing the background material to the back or bottom of the shadow box.

Next, center the pattern and glue it down. Or if you prefer, you can just draw the pattern from a stencil or freehand.

While the glue is setting up, start preparing the jewelry you want to use. In order for the pieces to lie flat, you will have to take the attachments off the back of pins or earrings. If you are using a necklace or bracelet, you will need to separate the links.

After the glue is dry, start experimenting with laying out the jewelry on the pattern. This can be done in whatever random order you like. I like my memory board to have balance; if I'm using a pair of earrings, for example, I will put one on each side of the piece in approximately the same location.

Once you have a general arrangement in mind, start gluing the jewelry to the pattern piece by piece. Try to stay within the lines of the pattern. It helps to have large and small pieces. The goal is to cover the entire face of the pattern with some type of jewelry. You can also use stones or seed pearls.

As this love keepsake takes shape, you will be surprised how soothing it is to put together. It is a simple but elegant reminder of your loved one that you can display anywhere. To me, just the gathering of these items that represent my love of Gordon was a blessing.

Gordon's memory box. A memory box is a great way to display treasured mementos of your loved one.

Letter from Gordon

Sweetheart,

Thank you so much for all of the letters. It sounds as though your life has gone on. And, honey, I'm very proud of the decisions that you've made, especially those about the house and motor home. Sounds as if you're still enjoying what we started with our traveling.

Yes, you're right, we have been encouraging you to write your books. Our story can help other people get through some of life's worst obstacles. I know how hard it was for you to quit your job to do this, but the journey you've begun and the continuing objectives are projects you were destined to do. All we did was nudge you along.

I'm very glad that you have found someone new in your life. I know that Doug has been supportive of you, just as I was always supportive of whatever decisions you made in your life. And yes, you still have beauty, purpose, talent, and a heart full of love.

Forever your love,
Gordon

Conclusion

Sometimes I feel like a newscaster. It seems like the subjects that I write about are difficult for you, the reader, to read. And yet, in order to get anyone to "tune in," there has to be some good news interspersed with the bad.

In *The Losing of Gordon,* the good news is that you can get through your grief. You can rebuild from tragedy with the tools that you have accumulated all your life. A broken shell still has beauty and purpose. You did not ask for your rebirth, but it will transport you into your future life.

Writing letters like the ones before the chapters in this book can be a somewhat healing activity. It's almost like you have opened a new connection (of sorts) with your loved one. If you decide to try it, you should be prepared for the emotional impact. I was shocked at how hard it was, even with the three-year gap since I lost Gordon. There are actually some grief Web sites that recommend it.

The goal of *The Saving of Gordon* was to take the reader through the fight to find the right treatment and support for a loved one during a cancer battle. *The Losing of Gordon* is meant to help those who have lost loved ones move on with their life, whether the loss is from cancer or another cause. While both of these books have different purposes, they have two common threads: Gordon and Joni. We both traveled on the same path that we chose, then on separate paths that we could not control.

One thing is certain: I have become a better person for having known, loved, helped, lost, and mourned for Gordon. No, we weren't perfect. Yes, we made mistakes in our lives. But I will never regret one single moment that I spent with Gordon. My hope is that our stories will both inspire you and enlighten you wherever your future leads.

May God bless you and your family while you travel on this earth, and may you give of yourself to help others, which will lead your heart to peace and your soul to personal growth.

Index

Made in the USA
Charleston, SC
21 December 2009